Reforging
the Central Bank

The Top-Level Design of the
Chinese Financial System in the New Normal

Series on Chinese Economics Research*

(ISSN: 2251-1644)

Series Editors: Yang Mu *(Lee Kuan Yew School of Public Policies, NUS)*
Fan Gang *(Peking University, China)*

Published:

Vol. 6: People's Livelihood in Contemporary China:
Changes, Challenges and Prospects
edited by Li Peilin

Vol. 7: New Paradigm for Interpreting the Chinese Economy:
Theories, Challenges and Opportunities
by Justin Lin Yifu

Vol. 8: Economic Transition in China:
Long-Run Growth and Short-Run Fluctuations
by Yuan Zhigang

Vol. 9: Opening Up China's Markets of Crude Oil and Petroleum Products:
Theoretical Research and Reform Solutions
by Sheng Hong and Qian Pu

Vol. 10: Administrative Monopoly in China: Causes, Behaviors and Termination
by Sheng Hong, Zhao Nong and Yang Junfeng

Vol. 11: The Ecology of Chinese Private Enterprises
by Feng Xingyuan, Christer Ljungwall and He Guangwen

Vol. 12: Game: The Segmentation, Implementation and Protection of
Land Rights in China
by Zhang Shuguang

Vol. 13: Social Integration of Rural-Urban Migrants in China:
Current Status, Determinants and Consequences
by Yue Zhongshan, Li Shuzhuo and Marcus W Feldman

Vol. 14: Reforging the Central Bank: The Top-Level Design of the
Chinese Financial System in the New Normal
by Haiqing Deng and Xi Chen

*For the complete list of volumes in this series, please visit
www.worldscientific.com/series/scer

Series on Chinese Economics Research – Vol. 14

Reforging the Central Bank

The Top-Level Design of the Chinese Financial System in the New Normal

Haiqing DENG

CITIC Securities, China

Xi CHEN

CITIC Securities, China

社会科学文献出版社

SOCIAL SCIENCES ACADEMIC PRESS (CHINA)

 World Scientific

Published by

World Scientific Publishing Co. Pte. Ltd.

5 Toh Tuck Link, Singapore 596224

USA office: 27 Warren Street, Suite 401-402, Hackensack, NJ 07601

UK office: 57 Shelton Street, Covent Garden, London WC2H 9HE

Library of Congress Cataloging-in-Publication Data
Names: Deng, Haiqing, author.
Title: Reforging the Central Bank : the top-level design of the Chinese financial system in the
    new normal / Haiqing Deng and Xi Chen (CITIC Securities, China).
Description: New Jersey : World Scientific, 2016. |
    Series: Series on Chinese economics research ; Vol 14
Identifiers: LCCN 2015031780 | ISBN 9789814704793 (alk. paper)
Subjects: LCSH: Banks and banking--China. | Financial institutions--
    Law and legislation--China. | Monetary policy--China.
Classification: LCC HG3336 .D46 2016 | DDC 332.1/10951--dc23
LC record available at http://lccn.loc.gov/2015031780

British Library Cataloguing-in-Publication Data
A catalogue record for this book is available from the British Library.

《再造央行：新常态下的中国金融顶层设计》
Originally published in Chinese by Social Sciences Academic Press
Copyright © Social Sciences Academic Press 2014

In-house Editors: Dipasri Sardar/Qi Xiao

Typeset by Stallion Press
Email: enquiries@stallionpress.com

Printed in Singapore

Contents

Introduction: From "The Old Normal" to "The New Normal"

"The New Normal" became a catchphrase in 2014. This term was first put forward by President Xi Jingping in May 2015 during his inspection trip to central China's Henan Province. He said, "since China is still at a critical period of strategic opportunities, we need to have more faith in ourselves. We should adapt ourselves to the New Normal and stay sober in terms of strategies based on the characteristics of our current development stage." The ensuing in-depth report from *People's Daily*, *CCTV News* and other official media along with the heated discussion in the financial market helped clarify the meaning of this term. Xi later in the APEC Summit in November 2014 described the basic features of the New Normal as "a shift from high to medium-to-high speed growth, economic optimization and structural upgrades, and a shift from investment to innovation as the driving force for growth." He also elaborated on the "overlapping of three periods," namely "the transition period of growth rate, the throes period for structural adjustment, and the digestion period for early-stage stimulus policies."

Earlier in 2009, Pacific Investment Management Company (PIMCO) used "The New Normal" to describe the recovering period of the world economy following the financial crisis, which was characterized by slow economic growth and low interest rate in most countries.

It should be noted that "The New Normal" at home and abroad are different.

First, they differ in essence. The New Normal in China in nature is a "transition period" where economic growth, structure and drivers undergo permanent changes and we will not go back to the Old Normal. In contrast, the global New Normal is more of a "recovering period" which is the slow growth period between two periods of regular growth. The New Normal will be followed by the Old Normal.

Second, they differ in time frames. The New Normal in the West began in the wake of the financial crisis whereas China's New Normal surfaced around 2013; the American New Normal will probably come to an end in 2015, the year when China is in the height of the New Normal and will stay so for years or even decades.

The opening part of the book — from "The Old Normal" to "The New Normal" — includes two chapters. The first chapter is about China's "Old Normal" and operational logics of the Central Bank; the second one is about China's "New Normal" and the Central Bank's problems and challenges.

Chapter One

"The Old Normal" and China's Central Bank

SECTION ONE: CHINA'S ECONOMIC FEATURES IN "THE OLD NORMAL"

In 2014, the financial market followed China's "New Normal" closely while the "Old Normal" attracted little attention. For one thing, many considered themselves "veterans" who had lived and therefore understood the "Old Normal," and no further study was needed. For another, the "Old Normal" was "in the past tense" with little value for research. However, I hold that the research on the "Old Normal" is significant. Only by figuring out the economic pattern and the Central Bank's operational logics will we be able to understand the Chinese economy and the Central Bank in the "New Normal." Or rather, only by learning the defects of the "Old Normal" will we be able to identify the reform direction in the "New Normal."

For example, the Old Normal was plagued by "soft intervention" which was a great barrier to the liberalization of China's interest rate. The government will undoubtedly take measures to remove this obstacle in the New Normal. In early 2014 way before the market followed New Normal, I argued that "the hardening of soft intervention," most probably through centralized management of local governments' debts and government

1

performance evaluation, was a major issue in interest liberalization (in his article "De Facto Default Cannot Save China's Debt Market" published on March 7th). In the second half of 2014, the central and subnational governments rolled out relevant policies, the milestone of which was "Opinions of the State Council on Strengthening the Administration of Local Government Debt." This document, released in October 2014, offered a comprehensive solution to local governments' debt problems. Hence, my prediction became a reality.

Here is another example. Balance of payments, one of the Central Bank's four monetary policy "targets," is closely related to the unilateral appreciation of renminbi (RMB) in the Old Normal. We can therefore predict the Central Bank's choices against the Impossible Trinity in the Old Normal and further predict the policy shift of the Bank in the New Normal.

As far as I am concerned, the features of the "Old Normal" includes, first, economic growth driven by infrastructure construction and real estate investment; second, high synchronization of five cycles and strong trends; third, GDP-dominated macro control, other goals centering around GDP growth; fourth, unilateral rising of real estate prices; fifth, unilateral appreciation of RMB.

The following paragraphs will discuss: first, growth pattern and real estate prices; second, macro control and the synchronization of the five cycles. The features of the Old Normal mentioned above will also be covered.

Growth Pattern and Real Estate Prices

Michael E. Porter in *The Competitive Advantage of Nations* classifies the development of nations' competitiveness into four stages: factor-driven stage, investment-driven stage, innovation-driven stage and wealth-driven stage. The investment-driven stage and the innovation-driven stage are wide apart. In contrast, the spacing between the factor-driven stage and the investment-driven stage and that between the innovation-driven stage and the wealth-driven stage are relatively small; most countries could go through the transition naturally. In light of this, the author holds that economic growth patterns can be simply put into two categories: one is investment-driven pattern, the other is innovation-driven pattern. Shifting from the investment-driven pattern to the innovation-driven pattern marks a country's success in overcoming the middle-income trap and becoming a developed economy.

In the Old Normal, China's economy was largely driven by infrastructure construction and real estate investment featured by government-dominated growth. It should be noted that "largely" does not imply that infrastructure construction and real estate investment accounted for over 50% of China's GDP; it only means that their share of China's GDP was higher than that in developed countries and that the two of them combined could literally shape China's economic cycle. For example, in the wake of the financial crisis in 2008, the government initiated the "Four Trillion" stimulus package, the bulk of which went into infrastructure investment. Soon, the real estate sector began to recover, breathing life into the heavy industry. Another example was the end of 2012 when the economy began to pick up. Likewise, infrastructure construction and real estate investment were the first to recover, and drove other sectors.

Now we will discuss the features of infrastructure construction investment and the real estate industry.

Infrastructure construction investment drove the economy in the following ways. First, investment itself could directly generate GDP; second, infrastructure construction investment produced huge demand for manufactured goods and the expanding reproduction of the manufacturing sector produced GDP; third, such investment created favorable environment and conditions for economic development which accommodated the development of all sectors, a phenomenon known as *the multiplier effect*; fourth, infrastructure construction investment was government-dominated and counter-cyclical whereas other sectors such as the consumption were market-driven and pro-cyclical. This follows that when the economy went down, infrastructure construction investment became an important hedge against economy slowdown and a major force to turn the economy around.

The primary defect of infrastructure construction investment was that since the government was the absolute leader of investment, the scale and efficiency of investment were not determined by the market; the strong political influence gave rise to pronounced repercussions and uncertainties.

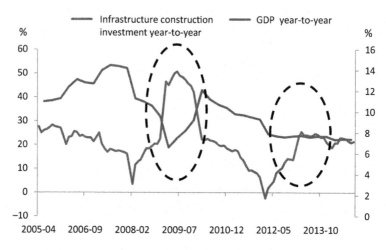

Figure 1.1 "Counter-cyclical" infrastructure construction offers great support to the economy. (Citation: WIND)

Infrastructure construction investment has significant repercussions. The repercussion of governmental stimulus was the leading driving force of China's economic cycle. For instance, if all of a sudden the government released a large stimulus package, the demand for manufactured goods would skyrocket. Relatively liberalized markets such as concrete and steel would see expanding capacities in no time. However, when the investment wave subsided, the newly built capacities were just up and running. Declining demand for manufactured goods coupled with oversupply led to excessive overcapacity. Moreover, the corporate exit mechanism was underdeveloped in China. SOEs' domination of capacities is largely unmarketized, because of the need to avoid large unemployment and provide a *weiwen environment* (stability maintenance); businesses are hard to go bankrupt, which aggravated the problem. As a result, China's PPI has remained negative since 2011.

The uncertainty of infrastructure construction investment is three-fold.

First, the appropriateness of scale was uncertain. The government had trouble deciding the scale of a stimulus plan. If too small, the stimulus would not turn the economy around; if too large, the economy might suffer short-term overheating and long-term stagnation.

Second, the appropriateness of investment areas was uncertain. The investment project intended to boost growth might be put in the wrong

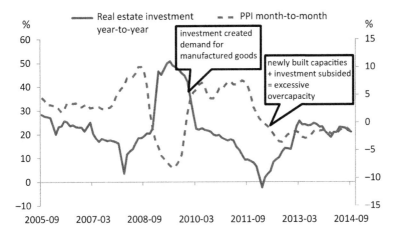

Figure 1.2 Repercussion of infrastructure construction investment — persistent negative PPI.

place. Investment aimed at sustaining growth was usually an emergency treatment without thorough planning. All this haste might result in low efficiency or failure.

Third, the effectiveness of local governments' implementation was uncertain. Local governments' actions were not under the full control of the central government. One scenario was when "the policy is confined to the State Council," or the central government exerted limited influence on local governments. Another scenario was that local governments only pretended to follow central policies by forging information and actually did otherwise. Given the multiple uncertainties around infrastructure investment, the effects of the government's massive infrastructure investment were highly uncertain and the aftermath of the "Four Trillion" and thus the economic slowdown after 2012 took the government by surprise.

I believe that it is reasonable and necessary for a developing country to boost economy through investment in infrastructure construction, especially when the economy glides down. However, the intensity, direction and method of investment should be taken into thorough consideration. In terms of intensity, overstimulation should be avoided; in terms of direction, investment industries and areas should be chosen with discretion; in terms of method, effective supervision mechanism should be put in place to make sure the money is well spent. Infrastructure investment used to play a critical role in China, but it will eventually fade out or survive in a new form, such as the "Chinese version of Marshall Plan," a catchphrase at the end of 2014.

Real estate was the second most important driving force in the Old Normal Chinese economy. It bore similarities as well as differences with infrastructure investment. Real estate investment created huge demand for manufactured goods as did infrastructure investment, making it a downstream industry of heavy industry. It differs from infrastructure investment in that: first, real estate was not completely government-led, or rather, the government preferred indirect measures such as land supply and policy adjustment over direct investment and price intervention; second, having no multiplier effect, real estate investment was more of a financial asset; third, real estate cycle, smoother and longer, was closely related to prices and trading volume. The fact that current month chain price index and trading volume were primary indicators of real estate investment testified that this industry was much more liberalized.

In retrospect, despite cyclical fluctuations in prices, the duration and range of increase were more significant than those of decrease. Therefore, the price change could be considered as unilateral increase. The rise began in 1998 when housing system reform kicked in and accelerated in 2004 with the introduction of the bid invitation, auction and listing system with only two brief drops in 2008 and 2012. According to statistics from State Statistics Bureau, the national average price was 2,050 yuan per square meter in 1999, 2,700 in 2004 and 5,800 in 2012; it rose by 110% from 2004 to 2012, with an annual growth rate of 10%. In Beijing, the average price was 5,600 yuan per square meter in 1999, 5,050 in 2004 and 17,000 in 2012; it rose by over 240% from 2004 to 2012, with an annual average growth rate of over 16%. For reference, the CPI base was 432 in 1999, 456 in 2004 and 580 in 2012; it rose by only 27% from 2004 to 2012, with an average increase rate of a mere 3%.

The rise of CPI was far slower than that of real estate prices

A lot has been said about the rising house prices, mainly about the supply and demand.

On the supply side, commercial residential houses were mainly supplied by real estate companies while affordable houses and self-built

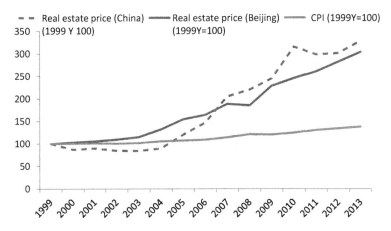

Figure 1.3   From 2004 on, house prices rose way faster than CPI. (Citation: WIND).

houses took only a small share. Since the certification of real estate companies was under strict regulation, the market was in some way a monopoly market. When the cost rose, real estate companies would undoubtedly pass on the burden to consumers, pushing up the house prices. The cost of real estate companies includes land cost, labor cost and building material cost, the third being related to the capacity and cycle of manufactured goods. I will now elaborate on the land cost and labor cost. First, considering land cost, the Land Administration Law provides that the nation in line with the law could requisition or expropriate land and offer compensation while any organization or individual must apply to the government for construction land, which makes the government the sole supplier of land and the monopoly of land rights. In result, the pricing of land was to a great degree up to the government. As land-selling revenue was a major part of local governments' fiscal revenue, those governments were more than willing to see the price rise. Second, labor cost began to surge around 2006 as China passed the Lewis Turning Point where labor supply came into shortage. Real estate companies passed on the rising labor cost to consumers, pushing up house prices.

Demand can be discussed in two categories: investment demand and consumption demand. First, investment demand derived from expectations for rising house prices based on experiences and the faith that local governments would rescue the market given their excess dependence on land revenue. The rising house prices propped up expectations for further increase, creating a positive feedback loop that stimulated demand for investment. The loose monetary policy from 2009 to 2010 contributed to corporate and individual wealth. Real estate, whose value is easy to preserve and increase, became the optimal investment choice. Prior to 2013, investment demand in real estate mainly came from four groups: Wenzhou professional speculators, coal mine owners from Shanxi, the second generation of the rich or the politicians and international hot money. Second, consumption demand was linked to housing system reform, urbanization, demographics, increasing income, traditions, underdeveloped affordable housing system and *hukou*, to name just a few. After the housing system reform, the long depressed consumption demand exploded, a precondition for the rising price. Urbanization began to speed up after 1996, with urbanization rate rising from 29% to 54% from 1995 to 2013; the shift in the demographic profile also gave rise to house demand. The period between 1980 and 1987 marked the peak of new births. Given that inelastic demand comes from the 25-to-30-year-olds, 2004 stood to be the year of accelerating price rise. Since 2004, urban per capita disposable income has maintained a year-on-year growth rate of over 10%. The rise of income was the prerequisite for the release of inelastic demand. In Chinese tradition, renting an apartment is only temporary while buying a house is a must for marriage. Hence the saying "mothers-in-law are the culprits of high house price." China is yet to develop a functional affordable housing system. In consequence, some inelastic demand that should have been covered by the government was handled through the market, leaving the real estate market over-liberalized. Some cities grant *hukou* only to those with houses, pushing up inelastic demand.

In a nutshell, supply was monopolized by the government and real estate companies, while consumption demand and investment demand continued to rise. The surge in house prices was inevitable. Despite multiple attempts to discipline the market, the government never tried to address the supply–demand imbalance. Without addressing the root cause, more policy changes would only lead to further increase. That is why real estate prices have, against all these policy changes, risen to a point where the public could not take it anymore.

The continuous increase in house prices had two critical effects: first, it made the real estate industry and relevant manufacturing industries the pillars of China's growth; second, it led to continuous rise of interest rate, excruciating industries that were not relevant to the real estate.

First, during the two gold periods for real estate — from 2006 to 2008 and from 2010 to 2011 — investment in real estate rose by 35% whereas investment in fixed assets rose only by 25%. Real estate over-expansion gave temporary vitality to industries with overcapacity and thus contributed to the economy. However, after 2011, the growth of real estate investment dropped to 20% and lower and thus the demand for steel diminished and concrete exacerbated overcapacity. The Chinese economy embarked on a downward path.

Second, blessed with higher-than-normal profitability, the real estate could take on higher return rate, making it a magnet of capital. Before 2011, given the unduly loose monetary policy during the "Four Trillion" period, there was no distinct sign of real estate squeezing capital out of other industries. 2011 saw a drop of M2 growth and the competition for capital reserves intensified. The year 2012 witnessed the boom in "non-standardized assets." As a bourgeoning power, banks' wealth management services provided an alternative to the previously rigid capital low channels. Such a change was in nature one step forward toward interest liberalization. However, due to the various distortions in the market, excess capital kept flowing into real estate and yields of bonds, in particular, state bonds, skyrocketed. The aftermath was the biggest bear market of bonds since 2004. The cost of corporate bill financing and bond financing rose sharply and loan interest also saw mild increase, further elbowing out other industries, especially private businesses. This might have led to Prime Minister Li Keqiang's multiple calls for lowering cost of private financing in 2014.

Despite the different features listed above, real estate and infrastructure construction were closely linked. This is why I put them in the same section. First, the capital source for infrastructure investment was connected with land revenue. 30% to 50% (subject to variations in statistical caliber, such as central transfer payment) of local finance came from government funds (largely land-selling revenue), making real estate-related revenue a major source of infrastructure investment. Meanwhile, a chunk of real estate price was land cost. According to Ren Zhiqiang, Chairman of Huayuan Property, land cost takes up almost 50% of the selling price; given the low price elasticity of demand resulted from the state's full control of land, individual purchases of house could be interpreted as investment in infrastructure (Ren Zhiqiang, "Land Cost and Taxes Push Property Price up 70%," *The Beijing Youth Daily* 2011). In addition, real estate relied on infrastructure investment. Without functional infrastructure, the value of commercial houses will shrink; properties near subway or high-speed rail were sold at higher prices. In general, real estate and infrastructure investment were interdependent, a joint force that drove the economy in the Old Normal.

Macro Control and Synchronization of the Five Cycles

I believe that GDP-domination was the guideline of the central government's macro control in the Old Normal. Local governments even regarded GDP as the sole touchstone for their performance. As a result, futile investment projects intended to boost GDP were commonplace and inefficient model of growth led to the wastage of resources and environmental pollution, which could jeopardize growth sustainability. This problem became acute during economic slowdown where the macro control was a chess game and GDP the king. "Stimulus" was the most important measure and had even become a byword for macro control in the Old Normal. As discussed above, stimulus led by infrastructure investment has defects — strong repercussions and uncertainties. Intensive stimulus always marks the beginning of an economic cycle in the Old Normal.

In the Old Normal, growth cycle, real estate bubble cycle, funds outstanding for foreign exchange cycle, inflation cycle and capital cost cycle were highly synchronized and subject to volatile fluctuation. In the Old Normal, economic downturn was mostly triggered by exterior impact. Under the GDP-domination mentality, the government adopted progressive fiscal policy and loose monetary policy to bolster the economy. The National Development and Reform Commission (NDRC) approved many projects, injecting huge amount of investment capital into infrastructure. The surge of money supply pushed up demand for manufactured goods followed by economic recovery and a price rise in manufactured goods.

Due to the expectations of RMB appreciation, when the economy showed signs of recovery, waves of hot money would swarm in. Being risk-lover, the hot money mostly flew into real estate and the stock market, further boosting these two markets. Upon completion of infrastructure projects, local governments preferred to borrow new money to pay the debt rather than pay off the principal, an action that kept financing demand high. With high financing demand and incoming hot money, when the economy began to recover, the central bank had difficulty withdrawing currency and as a result, money supply continued to rise. When the economy became overheated, high inflation and real estate bubbles coexisted, pushing up capital cost instantly. Since the actual growth rate had surpassed potential growth rate and high interest rate had stopped companies from further leveraging, fast growth could no longer be sustained. Once hit by external shock, the economy would turn a U-turn until the next round of stimulus.

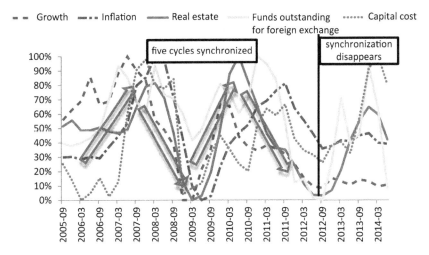

Figure 1.4 In the "Old Normal," five cycles (growth cycle, real estate bubble cycle, funds outstanding for foreign exchange cycle, inflation cycle and capital cost cycle) were synchronized; in the "New Normal," the synchronization disappears. (Citation: WIND)

Note: In Figure 1.4, the growth rate is the quarter-on-quarter GDP growth, inflation the month-on-month CPI growth, house price the month-on-month price change of 70 big-and-middle cities, funds outstanding for foreign exchange the moving average of 5 months' new outstanding funds in the central bank caliber and interest rate the return rate of 10-year state bonds. All the statistics are quarterly averages from the third quarter of 2005 to the second quarter of 2014. All the statistics, being in the above timeframe, have been normalized to [0, 100%].

The time between 2009 and 2012 was a complete cycle of Old Normal. Following the financial crisis in 2008, China's double-digit growth dropped to 6.6%. To reverse the economic downturn, the government resorted to strong fiscal stimulus and loose monetary policy, which gave birth to the "Four Trillion" investment plan. Back then, NDRC and the Ministry of Finance played a leading role in macro control. As huge amount of capital was waiting to be released, the two departments approved many investment projects, including those that had been previously rejected. The central bank adopted loose monetary policy and offered window guidance to credit line, putting excess capital in banks. Credit clerks had no choice but to offer capital to companies to meet their quotes. During this process, companies became the final destination of the money. In the early days of the stimulus, most of the capital was invested in infrastructure by the government, but somewhere in the middle, the money flew into the real estate. In mid-2009, infrastructure investment grew by 50% while in the third quarter of 2010, real estate saw investment rise by up to 40%. With a set of stimulus measures, the year-on-year GDP growth rate climbed from 6.6% in the first quarter of 2009 to 12.6% in the fourth quarter of 2009 and maintained at over 10% in 2012. It stood as the chief engine for global economic recovery.

When the economy was set on the right path, funds outstanding for foreign exchange in 2009 grew by 200 billion yuan and showed signs of further increase. Meanwhile, house prices rebounded after hitting the bottom and began to climb, with a year-on-year increase of 15% in mid-2010, faster than the average 7% before the crisis. Moreover, inflation intensified. PPI reached 5% in October 2010 and CPI even passed 6%. The economy was in a typical volatile state. Capital cost also showed pro-cyclical features as 10-year state bond interest rate rebounded from 2.5% in early 2009 to 3.6% in 2010 and reached 4% in 2011. Loan interest was about 5.8% in 2009 but jumped to 7.8% in 2011. Under the investment-driven model, the five cycles hit the bottom one after another and rebounded in the same time and soon became overheated.

However, GDP growth stayed at over 10% for only three quarters. In response to rising inflation, the central bank raised interest rate five times in less than a year from October 2010 to July 2011 until it came back to the pre-crisis level. Meanwhile, as new capacities intended to meet demand for steel and concrete created by the "Four Trillion" completed, a tsunami of manufacturing capacities were released. However, since the hyper-sized investment for infrastructure was unsustainable, demand plummeted, leaving overcapacity one major conundrum for the Chinese economy up to this day. Furthermore, high financing cost posed a huge burden on private companies who changed from leveraging to deleveraging, resulting in less demand. GDP growth went down since the third quarter in 2010 and reached 9.3% by 2011.

The above decrease in GDP growth might be considered natural as the hyper-investment normalized, a phenomenon that demanded little concern from the market. However, the 2011–2012 European debt crisis engulfed the whole of Europe with EU's GDP growth hitting bottom twice since 2011. Shrinking exports coupled with bleak expectation for the global economy dragged down China's unsustainably high growth, leaving China with a growth rate of 7.3% in the third quarter of 2012. In the meantime, the five cycles, namely, growth cycle, real estate bubble cycle, funds outstanding for foreign exchange cycle, inflation cycle and capital cost cycle, all went downward in 2012, which marked the completion of an Old Normal cycle. Looking back at the completed "Old Normal" cycle, the five cycles mutually reinforce each other in strong resonance, causing ups and downs in the economy.

The new economic cycle beginning in the third quarter of 2012 was different and can be treated as an incomplete Old Normal cycle and also the transition towards the New Normal. In this period, the economy was still driven by real estate and infrastructure construction and house price; interest rate and outstanding funds were still in synchronization. However, growth and inflation only fluctuated mildly with little sign of strong trends. Meanwhile, new features emerged in real estate prices and exchange rates, which will be discussed in the "New Normal" sections.

SECTION TWO: REVISITING "THE NEW NORMAL"

Since President Xi Jinping put forward "the New Normal," there has been a heated discussion in the market. At first, "the overlapping of three periods" was widely considered as the major characteristic of the New Normal, namely, "the transition period of growth rate, the throes period for structural adjustment, and the digestion period for early-stage stimulus policies." An article in *People's Daily* in August titled "The New Normal — How is it New?" summarized the four characteristics of the New Normal as "medium-to high-speed growth, up-graded economic structure, new economic drivers and multiple challenges." Xinwen Lianbo, CCTV's flagship news program, released a featured program of "New Normal, New Policies" which probes into the characteristics of the New Normal from multiple perspectives. Later, during the November APEC Summit, Xi clarified the basic characteristics as "a shift from high-speed to medium-to-high-speed growth, economic optimization and structural upgrades, and a shift from investment to innovation as the driving force for growth." Xi's summery of the New Normal is highly representative and authoritative, putting an end to the ongoing debate in the market. From then on, market interpretations of the New Normal have never deviated from Xi's summary; most of the efforts are devoted to data analysis and to the expansion and improvement of the three characteristics.

In my opinion, "the New Normal" is closely linked to interest liberalization and the transformation of the central bank's monetary policy framework. From this perspective, the difference between the New Normal and the Old Normal can be discussed from two aspects — internal and external. Internally, the growth model has shifted, the synchronization of the five cycles has weakened, the real estate has entered a new stage and the scale and structure of infrastructure construction have changed. Externally, balance of payment is different, so is the trend of RMB exchange rate.

Shift of Growth Model and Weakening of the Synchronization of the Five Cycles

In the Old Normal, factor-driven and investment-driven growth was the main characteristic; infrastructure construction and real estate investment were the direct driving forces of growth; RMB exchange rate appreciated unilaterally; "the fives cycles" — growth cycle, real estate bubble cycle, funds outstanding for foreign exchange cycle, inflation cycle and capital cost cycle — were highly synchronized. Back then, the government's macro control policy was managed as a chess game where all financial and monetary policies were centered on the "King" — GDP growth. This phenomenon has been discussed in the first section of this chapter.

In the New Normal, however, China has entered the innovation-driven and investment-driven growth stage. China's East is largely driven by innovation with consumption upgrading and the service sector as the major growth points while the East is the primary force of new type of urbanization with decreasing growth rate of investment. In the meantime, the export of infrastructure construction is becoming a new growth point; the real estate market will be more consumption-driven than investment-driven; the house price will be stable; RMB will no longer appreciate unilaterally and will undergo two-way fluctuation. In this period, macro control becomes a Go game (literal meaning: "encircling game") with targeted policies toward each objective.

Around 2014, China transformed from investment-driven model to innovation- and investment-driven model, which marks the main characteristic of the New Normal. In my opinion, in East cities and regions with high urbanization rate, demand for infrastructure investment has come down as urbanization there hits the bottleneck. However, in the West, there is still demand for more infrastructure construction and more rapid urbanization pace; the region is not ready for the innovation-driven model. Therefore, as far as I am concerned, "the new driver" of the New Normal means that the Chinese economy will no longer be driven by single force, be it factor of investment; rather it will be jointly driven by several forces with innovation included. In the New Normal, economic growth model will enter the post-industrial society stage featured by "regional differentiation and multiple drivers" with innovation the key variation to economy. In the Old Normal, the five cycles were highly synchronized while in the New Normal the five cycles will be subject to significant changes.

The growth cycle

Investment growth will be in a sustainable range without sudden surges that were common in the Old Normal. In 2013, infrastructure investment grew by 20% to 25% and real estate investment 10% to 20%. Investment becomes a "cushion" to China's economy rather than an "engine." Growth will be mostly driven by consumption and the service industry with innovation industry the highlight. Companies that are highly sensitive to financing cost will replace local governments and real estate companies numb to cost as the ones that promote growth. With rising interest rate, the corporate sector following the rule of market will downsize or exit, leaving the economy safe from overheating.

The real estate bubble cycle

In response to the financial crisis, unduly loose monetary policy was adopted. The resulting over-supply of currency coupled with an influx of hot money led to real estate bubble and high inflation. In the New Normal, however, monetary policy will be stable and prudent. More specifically, the amount of money in the economy will be kept at a proper level; macro control will target prices and be counter interest cycle so as to stabilize the economy. Moreover, it will be common for the government to protect inelastic demand and curb arbitrage demand, which means houses will be more of a consumption good than an investment project. On top of this, the government will propel affordable housing and upgrade shanty towns to lift people's living standards. Except for real estate policy changes caused by financial pressure, the possibility of reviving real estate bubble remains low.

The funds outstanding for foreign exchange cycle

One of the causes for the influx of hot money was the appreciating RMB caused by its substantial under-valuation. In 2014, the RMB exchange rate became relatively stable with two-way fluctuation. As a result, the inflow of arbitrage capital has plummeted and has shown ups and downs. Meanwhile, the central bank has withdrawn more from the routine intervention of foreign exchanges, leaving wider space for exchange rate fluctuation. The bank is also pushing for two-way fluctuation. In the first half of 2014, RMB depreciated by 4% against USD and appreciated 2% from May to August. Since May 2014, funds outstanding for foreign exchange grew by less than 100 billion yuan and even dropped by 90 billion yuan in June. As the central bank pushes for further exchange rate reform, funds outstanding for foreign exchange will be less effective as a means to inject base money and as an amplifier of the pro-economic cycle.

The inflation cycle

Each of China's past economic overheat was followed by high inflation with a lag phase of 1 to 2 years. Such a phenomenon was almost inevitable given China's reliance on huge money injection and the influx of hot money. Theoretically, for one reason, according to the Phillips curve, rapid growth (or low unemployment) is related to high inflation; for another, according to the equation $MV = PY$, where P (production) growth drops after a surge with MV unchanged, Y (prices) will go up. I think that high inflation could be divided into three short-term fluctuations — industrial goods related, household income related and fruit and vegetable. When the economy goes up, prices of manufactured goods will rise and household income will also increase significantly. So will the inflation. In the New Normal, China's economy will be subject to less cyclical fluctuation and inflation will only fluctuate within a narrow range. From 2012 to the day the book was written, CPI maintained between 2% and 3%, a major characteristic of inflation in the New Normal.

The capital cost cycle

Capital cost has a natural negative effect on economic cycle: when economy grows rapidly, interest rate rises and so does corporate financing cost, which cools down the economy. However, since capital cost is primarily determined by GDP (real growth rate) + CPI (commodity prices), when in the Old Normal GDP and CPI fluctuated, capital -cost would also become volatile. Furthermore, in the Old Normal, due to soft intervention, property bubble and the lack of risk evaluation, interest rate was subject to sectors that are insensitive to capital cost, squeezing out other sectors. In the New Normal, the less sensitive sectors are restricted, real estate bubble is under control and risk evaluation becomes more relevant. Now that interest rate is in the hands of sectors highly sensitive to capital cost, the reverse effect of capital cost on economic cycle will finally become clear, protecting the economy from overheating and high inflation and mitigating fluctuations of other cycles.

In a nutshell, the five cycles in the New Normal will no longer be subject to strong cyclical trends and fluctuation will be less volatile while structural problems become more prominent. Figure 1.4 in Section one demonstrates that the synchronization of the five cycles has disappeared.

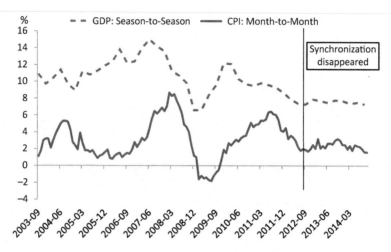

Figure 1.5 In "the New Normal" the synchronization of growth and inflation has disappeared. (Citation: WIND)

The economy used to be driven by infrastructure construction and real estate investment, but now the East is mainly driven by innovation while the West by investment. China is on the path away from the dilemma where less intervention leads to chaos but more leads to stagnation. In the New Normal, macro control becomes a Go game where multiple targets should be aimed at with tailor-made solution. The time when GDP plays the King has passed.

Next, I will talk about two issues: the house price entering the equilibrium zone and RMB exchange rate entering the equilibrium zone. The latter is the precondition for the transformation of the central bank's monetary policy framework while the former is important to interest rate liberalization.

Housing Price Entering Equilibrium Range and New Features of the Infrastructure

In the section on "the Old Normal," I analyzed the reasons that housing price previously rose unilaterally. In short, on the supply side, housing supply was monopolized by the government and real estate developers, and on the demand side, consumption demand and investment demand kept increasing, which, unavoidably, resulted in big rise of housing price. The government conducted multiple rounds of regulation and control, but never addressed the root cause — the imbalance between supply and demand. Instead of decreasing price, the regulation and control pushed it to a level unbearable for the general public.

Since April 2013, the month-on-month price increase of newly constructed houses in the 70 large and medium-sized cities of the National Bureau of Statistics started to fall, but still stood at 0.4% by December 2013. In 2014, the decrease of housing price speeds up. In July 2014, the month-on-month price increase plummeted to –0.9%, the lowest since statistics were available, and the year-on-year price increase dropped to 2.4%, the lowest since March 2014. As housing price dropped significantly, the real estate transaction volume also decreased markedly: for seven months from January to August 2014, 30 large and medium-sized cities saw negative year-on-year growth of commercial housing transaction area and decrease of both housing price and transaction volume.

Compared to the previous two drops (in 2008 and in 2012), this one has three differences: this round is not caused by policy regulation or external shock; the mutually reinforcing effects between housing price and people's income came to an end; the nature of real estate changed.

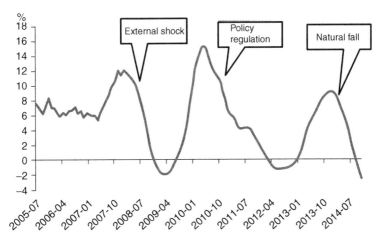

Figure 1.6 The three rounds of housing price drop are attributable to different causes. This round is not caused by external shock or policy regulation. (Citation: WIND)

This round of drop is endogenous, driven by market factors rather than policies or external shock. Reviewing the previous two rounds of drops, the 2008 one was caused by external shock while the 2012 one by real estate regulation and control. In short, they were both caused by factors beyond the real estate market, non-market factors. Housing price drop caused by non-market factors is not sustainable, that is, when supply and demand reach a certain threshold level, price will show a retaliatory rebound. 2013 saw no substantial change in real estate regulation. The new five regulations of 2013 basically failed, for example, regarding the accountability system, almost all regions failed to realize the regulation target, but none of them were held accountable. The real estate market of 2013 was basically a market-oriented one (except in Beijing, Shanghai and Guangzhou). Considering areas that saw price rise, previously it was high-end houses that rose in price. In 2013, it was the periphery of cities, which was a typical sign of rigid demand being released. Endogenous housing price drop under market conditions, compared with price drop caused by external shock or administrative intervention, is more sustainable.

The mutually reinforcing effects between housing price and people's income came to an end. Housing price and people's income used to have an obvious lagged correlation, reinforcing each other. For example, the month-on-month increase of housing price in December 2012 noticeably rebounded, and year-on-year growth of residents' disposable income in December 2012 reached a turning point; the month-on-month increase of housing price in January 2012 dipped to a low point, so did the year-on-year increase of residents' disposable income in June 2013. The two cycles reinforced each other, resulting in the alternate rise of housing price and disposable income. However, this round of housing price rise cycle is not followed by the year-on-year rise of disposable income. The possible reason is that housing price rise did not contribute to disposable income growth as this round of housing price rise is caused by the release of rigid demand, not investment price rise as in the past. The low year-on-year rise of disposable income will likely make this downward cycle of real estate price last longer than before and weaken the momentum for the next cycle of housing price rise.

The nature of real estate changed since house purchasers are different. In the past, real estate was mostly considered as investment. The feature

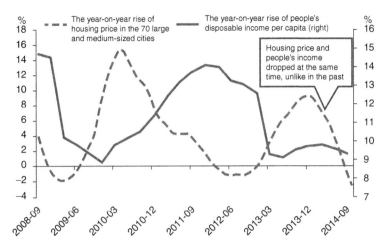

Figure 1.7   This time, housing price and people's income drop simultaneously instead of alternatively as in the past. (Citation: WIND)

of investment is that there exists a positive cycle: housing price rise → investment demand rise → housing price rise → investment demand rise. … Under such circumstances, pricing is not simply based on demand and supply as demand changes when price changes. As people make investments, they are concerned about the rise and fall of price, not the level of it. In 2013, major purchasers bought houses out of rigid demand, thus real estate changed from investment into general merchandise, thus the pricing returned to pricing based on supply and demand. As demand is released continuously and supply keeps increasing, oversupply will result in housing price drop. Considering house purchasers, previously they were mostly the large number of speculators from Wenzhen, the coalmine owners from Shanxi province, the second generation of officials and the rich, owners of international money. In 2013, their situation obviously changed. The rupture of capital chain left Wenzhen businessmen struggling. Coal price plummeting severely affected the coalmine owners of Shanxi. Amidst the anti-corruption campaign, the second generation of officials and the rich seldom buy domestic properties but prefer overseas ones. With the expectation of QE exit and stock price soaring in the United States, owners of international hot money withdrew from China's real estate market. As the major driving force shifts from investment to rigid demand, housing price stability is possibly now.

To sum up, I judge that real estate price has entered the equilibrium range mainly on the grounds of the changes in supply and demand. On the supply demand, the previous monopoly of real estate developers was broken up. Supply of houses in rundown areas that are renovated, affordable housing and low-rent housing started to increase, changing real estate pricing marginally; on the demand side, investment and speculative demand weakens, and people buy more houses for consumption demand; what is more, the turning point for rigid demand driven by the turning point of birth rate approaches. In addition, when a country's bubble burst, the enormous increase of rigid demand will be put to an end. Thus, it will be a long time before the foundation for forming bubbles emerges again. Rigid demand will hardly plunge as urbanization speeds up, and the government is unlikely to tolerate the crash of the real estate market, therefore I believe that the possibility for housing market crash is low and that the foundation for the housing bubbles to inflate no longer exists. This unprecedented market-driven housing price drop can be considered as the sign that housing price has entered the equilibrium range. Since June 2014, when Hohhot relaxed the restrictions on home purchases, every city, except Beijing, Shanghai, Guangzhou, Shenzhen and other megacities, among the 46 cities that impose restrictions on home purchases, has relaxed the restrictions. At the same time, housing loan policies have also been adjusted. Because of this, the month-on-month decrease of housing price started to become smaller in September and the year-on-year decrease of transaction volume started to recover in July. However, by October 2014, the year-on-year growth of both housing price and transaction area remained negative. I believe that the relaxation of measures such as restrictions on home purchases is the necessary trend for the real estate market to develop properly as the real estate market repressed by policies is not really market-based. Since the restrictions were relaxed, however, the newly increased demand remains consumption demand rather than investment demand, not changing the fact that supply and demand in the real estate industry is basically in overall balance and that housing price has entered in an equilibrium range.

Closely related to real estate, investment in infrastructure also showed some new features in 2014. First, overall investment growth in infrastructure dropped to 15–20% in the second half of 2014, and this figure was

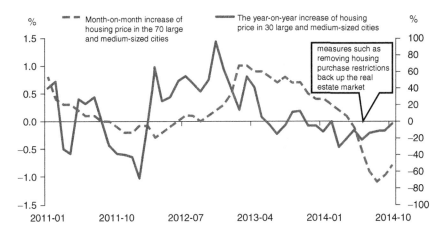

Figure 1.8 Removal of housing purchase restrictions led to smaller decreases of both housing price and sales. (Citation: WIND)

over 20% previously. Growth slowdown of investment in infrastructure is related to multiple factors, including slower growth of national fiscal income, weakened investment impulse of local governments after clean-government building efforts, less revenue from land sales in a sluggish real estate market, the shift of areas needing new infrastructure from the whole country to backward areas and so on. Second, investment in infrastructure turns to external demand such as export of high-speed railway, aiming at addressing overcapacity through technological upgrading. The future direction for infrastructure can be seen from various events ranging from Premier Li Keqiang's promotion of high-speed railway during almost every overseas visit and the establishment of BRICS Bank and Asia Infrastructure Investment Bank to "China's Marshall Plan" and so on.

Housing price entering the equilibrium range and the transformation of investment in infrastructure are of great significance for the liberalization of interest rates. The bubble-like increase of housing price and the shortage of discipline for local government debts will hugely disturb the financial market. More market-oriented interest rates and exchange rates lead to faster flow of capital from the society to real estate and faster inflation of bubbles, which will result in stronger crowding-out on other industries and more difficulties in economic restructuring. Reviewing interest rate liberalization of all countries, financial institutions' greater appetite for risks is the commonality. In China, the concern for the repayment capabilities of private enterprises is very grave, even to the point of being discriminate. It is impossible for commercial banks to lower their qualification requirements for enterprises. Thus real estate became the best investment target of capital, which was the most obvious in 2013. As housing price enters the equilibrium range and the discipline for local governments becomes stricter, financial institutions' preference for real estate and infrastructure will subside, which makes possible the optimization of financial resources, providing an opportune timing for pushing forward interest rate liberalization.

RMB Exchange Rate Entering the Equilibrium Range

On July 21, 2005, the People's Bank of China (PBOC) announced that China started to adopt a managed floating exchange rate regime based on market supply and demand with reference to a basket of currencies and that RMB would no longer be pegged to the US dollar and the RMB exchange rate regime will be improved with greater flexibility. RMB started to appreciate unilaterally and this appreciation lasted until the end of 2013 with the years 2008 and 2012 being exceptions. Judging by the central parity of US dollar against RMB, we find that the RMB exchange rate appreciated accumulatively by 26% by December 31, 2013.

The situation described above started to change during February to April 2014 when RMB exchange rate saw the biggest depreciation in the history. Judging by the exchange rate record since 2014, RMB against US dollars went through obvious two-way volatility. I believe that RMB exchange rate has entered an equilibrium range and will very likely continue to experience two-way volatility based on the following reasons: (1) the central bank has made it clear that it would withdraw from routine intervention, and this can only be implemented after RMB enters the equilibrium range; (2) considering the proportion of trade balance to GDP, there exists no condition for China's exchange rate to continue to appreciate by a large margin; (3) judging by purchasing parity, the degree to which RMB is underestimated is acceptable; (4) judging by the potential domestic and overseas interest rate arbitrage, the potential arbitrage based on both forward interest rate and spot exchange rate is falling to a

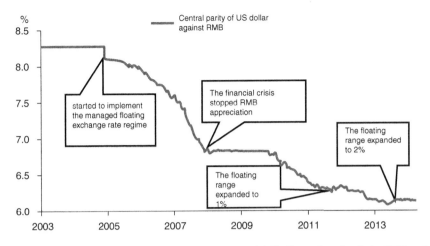

Figure 1.9   By 2014, the unilateral appreciation of RMB discontinued only in 2008 and 2012. (Citation: WIND)

low level; (5) foreign currency increases and funds outstanding for foreign exchange decreases, indicating a stronger readiness of enterprises and residents to hold foreign currency. The expectation for unilateral appreciation has been shattered. The two-way fluctuation has basically taken shape.

The central bank withdrew from routine intervention. There are two major pieces of evidence. First, the statement on external balance in the implementation report of the central bank's monetary policy was changed. Before 2014, the section of major tasks for the next stage retained the statement of "maintaining the basic stability of RMB exchange rate at a reasonable and balanced level and promoting the basic balance of international payments;" in the first quarter of 2014, it was changed to "maintaining the basic stability of RMB exchange rate at a reasonable and balanced level," and the part of "promoting basic balance of international payments" was deleted. Before the second quarter of 2014, the abstract of the report contained such statements as "properly using instrument portfolio to manage and adjust the liquidity of the bank system based on international payments and supply and demand of liquidity"; in the second quarter of 2014, the phrase "international payment" was completely deleted from the report, indicating that balance of international payments is no

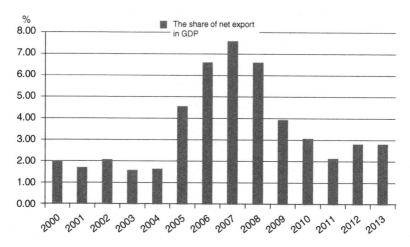

Figure 1.10   The proportion of trade balance to GDP fell to around 3%. (Citation: WIND)

longer the focus of PBOC. The second piece of evidence is that funds outstanding for foreign exchange position plunged starting from April 2014 and was basically zero or even negative from May to July. This showed that the central bank did in operation withdraw from intervening foreign exchange settlement and sale of commercial banks. I estimate that China's future growth of funds outstanding for foreign exchange will be kept around zero except when RMB exchange rate fluctuates violently.

The proportion of trade balance to GDP enters an equilibrium range. First, the judgment that RMB faces appreciation pressure based on trade balance being positive is flawed. This judgment is solid when trade balance dominates funds outstanding for foreign exchange, which results in huge pressure for inflow of foreign currency and thus an increasing demand for RMB that causes greater RMB appreciation. But when international hot money dominates funds outstanding for foreign exchange, the influence of trade balance on exchange rate will be weakened. From May to July 2014, China's trade had a balance of over RMB100 billion and funds outstanding for foreign exchange was zero or even negative. The outflow of hot money and the demand of enterprises and residents for foreign reserve served as a hedge against trade surplus. In addition, according to international common practices, trade balance accounting for less than 3% of GDP is considered at equilibrium. This proportion was over 5% from 2004 to 2008 and stands at around 2% from 2011 till now. The continuous fall of this proportion indicated that China's balance of payments has been improving and that China's economy is increasingly closer to balance with the external economy.

The implied exchange rate enters an equilibrium range. The theory of Purchasing Power Parity (PPP) says that the exchange rate is the ratio of the two countries' price level of tradable goods, or the ratio of purchasing power of the tradable goods of different currencies. PPP is the unit of a nation's currency needed to purchase in the domestic market goods and services equivalent to that purchased with one US dollar in the US. It also indicates the implied exchange rate. By comparing with the market exchange rate, we can get the deviation level of market rate to the implied exchange rate. The farther the ratio gets from 100%, the greater is the deviation. When the ratio is less than 1, the smaller the deviation, greater the underestimation of the exchange rate, and greater is the appreciation pressure. Vertically, China's deviation ratio in 2006 stood at about 35% and continued to grow close to 1. In 2015, the figure was already 57.2%, with a better-justified RMB exchange rate. Horizontally, developed countries in Europe and America enjoyed a deviation ratio around 100%, compared to which China still had a long way to go, but such a gap lies in the systematic differences between the developed and developing countries. In other words, free trade around the world is not applicable to all goods and services; income and consumption structures vary between developing and developed countries. Judged by deviation, China ranks among the middle in developing countries, and as I have observed, since the PPP theory is against considerable appreciation of RMB in a short term, it is difficult for China to raise the rate before it joins the league of developed countries.

Arbitrage opportunities narrow down significantly. Hot money floods into China for riskless arbitrage as interest rate in China is considerably higher than those in Europe and America, which further gives rise to pressure on a stronger RMB. Basically, there are two ways of engaging in riskless arbitrage: 1. Converting money borrowed from the US into RMB at spot exchange rate for riskless yields in China's market while using the forward exchange rate to cover exchange rate risks. 2. Converting the money into USD at the spot exchange rate when it flows out of China.

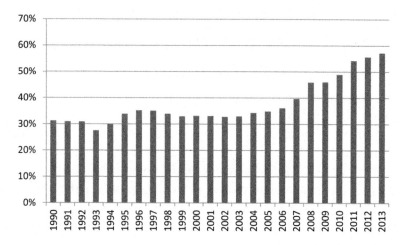

Figure 1.11   Real PPP exchange rate deviations in China. (Citation: WIND)

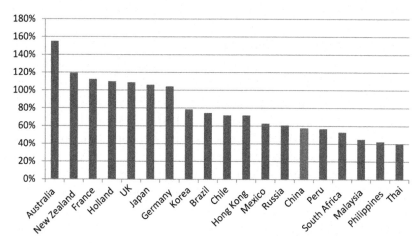

Figure 1.12   Real PPP exchange rate deviations in major countries. (Citation: WIND)

These two methods differ from each other in the hedging of exchange rate risks, which further determines the yields from exchange rate changes. The following diagram presents one-year yields out of the two models in terms of national debts with maturity of one year and 10 years. For those with maturity of one year, we assume they are held-to-maturity investments, while for those with maturity of 10 years, we assume the interest

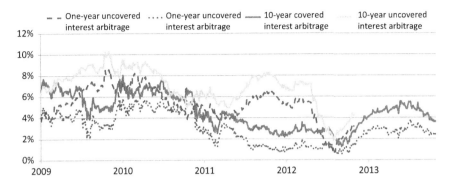

Figure 1.13 Yield estimates of riskless profits out of spreads between USD and RMB. (Citation: WIND)

rate to remain the same after one year, so there would be no capital gains. (This assumption is actually invalid. We can never accurately predict the interest rate one year ahead. But when we need to make decisions as to whether to invest money in China, such hypothesis is adoptable). As is shown in Figure 1.13, profits out of uncovered interest arbitrage are way outperformed by those from covered interest arbitrage. From 2009 to 2012, for uncovered interest arbitrage, profit margins are 6% and 7% respectively for the one-year and 10-year periods, much higher than yields from riskless asset investment abroad. On the other hand, covered interest arbitrage does not have as impressive performance, with profit margins respectively standing at 4% and 6% before 2012. After 2012, they continued to drop to about 2%, a level hardly acceptable to foreign hot money investors. Therefore, we can conclude that uncovered interest arbitrage is the dominant form after 2012. Yet it comes with exchange rate risks, which also explains the severe loss in international hot money investment after RMB appreciation in the first half of 2014. Behind uncovered interest arbitrage, arbitrageurs assume a unilateral appreciation of RMB, whereof exchange rate fluctuations only add to the profits without entailing any risks. Once the assumption loses ground, profits will plummet and pressure for inflow of hot money weakens, creating a positive feedback loop for RMB to reach equilibrium.

Expectation of bi-directional volatility replaces that of unilateral appreciation. As stated, with renewed expectation, the market will move toward a stable exchange rate spontaneously. Foreign exchange deposits

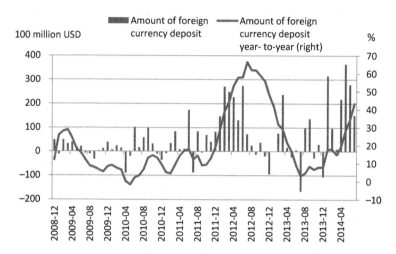

Figure 1.14   Amount of foreign currency deposit rebounds. (Citation: WIND)

rose tremendously starting from 2014, with a year-on-year increase of 40%, indicating a reversed expectation of unilateral appreciation from both the residents and businesses. Uncertain about the future exchange rate fluctuations, people deposit foreign currencies against possibilities of two-way volatility. Also, the self-fulfilling process of expectations facilitates the equilibrium of exchange rate.

Based on the aforementioned analysis, I think that exchange rate in China reached an equilibrium in 2014. However, these major characteristics were also observed in 2012. For example, the central bank emphasized in the 2012 executive report on monetary policy: "Demand and supply of foreign currency tends to strike a balance and further differentiation appears in terms of exchange rate expectations. RMB exchange rate will approach the equilibrium more than ever." At the same time, funds outstanding for foreign exchange in the central bank were around 0 and the ratio of balance of trade to GDP was within 3%. With the implied PPP exchange rate deviation almost the same as the current level, profit from covered interest arbitrage reached a historic low. In March 2012, Zhou Xiaochuan, Governor of People's Bank, said: "Now that RMB exchange rate has almost reached the equilibrium point, premier Li Keqiang gives special attention to the trend of a bi-directional floating regime." This shared much commonality with Yi Gang's words said in August 2014: "Net

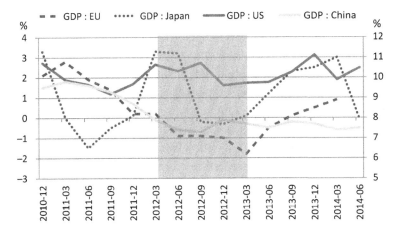

Figure 1.15   2012 GDP home and abroad. (Citation: WIND)

inflow of foreign exchange gradually got back to the equilibrium range." Also, the central bank adopted the same measure of expanding the range of exchange rate fluctuations in 2012 and 2014, driving a big rise in foreign currency reserve, breaking the unilateral appreciation expectation. However, such an expectation comes to dominate again after 2012.

With so many similarities between 2012 and 2014, was the equilibrium reached in 2012? If so, how did the unilateral appreciation expectation emerge again the following year? As far as I am concerned, there are four differences:

- Different international economic landscape. A significant drop (more than 1%) was observed in economic growth rate in the EU, Japan, and America from 2012 to the first half of 2013 with a mild one in China (only 0.4%). In such a context, exchange rate was pressurized to appreciate. In 2014, foreign economy embraces an extensive rebound while China's economy is very likely to remain stable, with certain downward risks, hence an unfavorable fundamental for great appreciation.
- Different monetary policies across the world. From 2012 to 2013, most countries abroad eased their monetary policies, America with QE3 in September 2012; Japan with super-quantitative easing in April 2014;

Europe with three interest cuts in July 2012 and in May and November 2013. These factors drove exchange rate in China to increase from the outward. In retrospect of the entire trend in China, turning points in RMB appreciation were observed in the aforementioned period. In June 2014, Europe started a package of loose monetary policies including a negative interest rate and directional long-term refinancing operations. That was also when exchange rate in China turned to appreciate again. Unlike 2012, the external environment has become too complicated to make prediction considering the imminent interest rate rise in America in 2015.

- Differences in domestic interest rate development. China's interest rate was at the bottom in 2012. The fourth quarter in 2012 and first quarter in 2014 both witnessed ongoing interest rate hikes with a great sore in the second half of 2013 as well, creating great arbitrage opportunities and attracting a huge inflow of hot money. But in 2014, interest rate stayed at a historic high with a likely downward trend, hence much less appeal to hot money.

- Different cycles for real estate sector. Such a difference has a huge impact upon hot money. After the second half of 2012, the housing sector entered a booming cycle which lasted a year, drawing an influx of hot money. On the other hand, as I have analyzed in the "New Normal," the spontaneous downward development in China's housing sector signified housing prices in equilibrium, which was essentially different from the slump due to administrative intervention in 2012.

In conclusion, I believe that the RMB exchange rate indeed reached an equilibrium in 2012 and the government's intervention played out its influence in the previous unilateral appreciation. However, due to the combined influence of a new round of monetary easing in developed countries, a high interest rate pressurized by the housing sector and financial system, and different monetary policies home and abroad, RMB was forced to embrace a new round of appreciation. Yet unlike before, this time, the market played a greater role. In 2014, factors home and abroad became more than complicated. Internationally, America was faced with an expected interest rate hike in 2015; Europe continued to ease monetary policy; Japan followed a bumpy path of economic development.

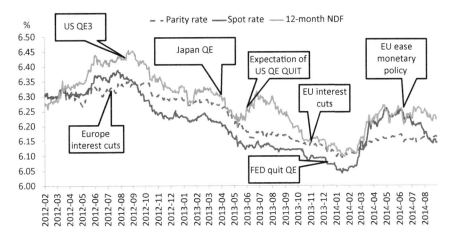

Figure 1.16   RMB exchange rate and monetary policies in developed countries. (Citation: WIND)

Domestically, the real estate sector hit a downward cycle together with huge downward risks for fundamentals. None of the conditions favored a unilateral appreciation of RMB.

An exchange rate in equilibrium is one of the most important features of China's New Normal and bears great strategic significance. It lays the foundation for a shift in monetary policies from central banks and facilitates a market-oriented interest rate and exchange rate. If RMB continues its unilateral appreciation with a market-based exchange rate, the appreciation will be significant, with huge inflow of international capital, rendering it impossible for an independent price-based monetary policy. If this happens, the central bank will be driven to adopt an exchange rate regime similar to the fixed ones and impose capital control. Therefore, exchange rate in equilibrium is significant for the shift of the central bank's monetary policy — from the quantitative to the price-based with the introduction of a liberalized capital account.

SECTION THREE: WHY ARE THE WAYS OF INJECTING BASE CURRENCY IMPORTANT?

In the Old Normal, the Central Bank of China bought foreign exchange in bulk. Funds outstanding for foreign exchange cycle were a major form for injecting base currency. Abroad, the major channel is open-market operation or deposit and loans from the central bank to commercial banks. The difference in ways of injecting base currency leads to significant difference in monetary policies and regulative measures.

In countries with liberalized interest rate, central banks use two tools to regulate the money market: open-market operation and interest rate corridor. In essence, both the methods are based on the model of "central bank to commercial banks," in which the central bank, working as the trading party of financial institutions, adjusts money supply and demand by modifying the scale of base currency injected or withdrawn. In consequence, the short-term interest rate is adjusted. The specific operation mechanism and differences between the two models will be elaborated in the chapter, "New Conduction Mechanism of Monetary Policy." For the sake of simplicity, the two methods of injecting base currency will be collectively referred to as open-market operations.

The two methods differ in: (1) variables of regulation, (2) targets for injection, (3) paths of circulation, and (4) influence on interest rate, which are discussed hereunder:

Different Variables of Regulation

Open-market operations modify both money supply and interest rate, while funds outstanding for foreign exchange cycle adjust money supply and exchange rate. In open-market operations, the central bank injects or withdraws base currency at a certain interest rate. Two variables are involved during the process: quantity and price for injection or withdrawal, which will influence base currency supply and interest rate. In injection of funds outstanding for foreign exchange cycle, the central bank directly purchases foreign exchanges, or the purchase is done indirectly through commercial banks. Two variables are involved during the process: quantity and price (exchange rate) of foreign exchange bought and sold, which will influence base currency supply and exchange rate. Consequently, open-market operations modify interest rate while injection of funds outstanding for foreign exchange cycle intervenes more on exchange rate.

Table 1.1 Differences in base currency injection

Ways of injection	Object of regulation	Risk preference
Open-market operation	Interest rate, supply of base currency	Low risk preference
Funds outstanding for foreign exchange cycle	Exchange rate, supply of base currency	High risk preference

Different Targets for Injection

Open-market operation targets banks and other money market players, while injection of funds outstanding for foreign exchange cycle targets residents, corporations, and international investors. Under the model of federal fund interest rate, the Federal Reserve modifies the amount of excess deposit reserves. Under the model of European interest rate corridor, the European central banks adjust the base currency in the overnight market. But with China's injection of funds outstanding for foreign exchange cycle, China's quantity of base currency is modified. The United States and Europe targeted banks, focused on short-term injection of base currency, in order to directly modify short-term interest rate. However, China's term of injection is uncertain; the actual targets are corporations, residents, and international investors. Therefore, short-term interest rate cannot be modified by injection.

Different Paths of Base Money Circulation

In open-market operations, base currency flows from the central bank to commercial banks, but the circulation of injected funds outstanding for foreign exchange cycle is more complicated. Specifically, when funds outstanding for foreign exchange cycle are the dominant form of injection, corporations, residents and international investors settle and convert foreign exchange into RMB through commercial banks. Commercial banks become foreign exchange holders, and then convert the exchange into RMB through the central bank. Ultimately, corporations, residents and international investors become base currency holders, and the central bank

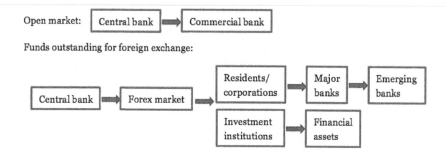

Figure 1.17　Different circulation paths of base currency under different injection models.

becomes a foreign currency holder. No changes occur in commercial banks' balance sheets. By doing so, the quantity of base currency held by corporations, residents and international investors is modified, but the injection does not influence commercial banks in the short term. Residents and corporations will deposit the earned base currency into banks as general deposit, which will influence the supply of broad money $M2$. However, international investors will invest the earned money in more risky financial assets, such as real estate, stock market, etc. When funds outstanding for foreign exchange cycle is the prevailing injection channel, whether banks can hold base currency depends on the scale of the bank and the layout of its branch. Major banks have advantages in that they have more branches and a reputation and hence convert more foreign exchanges. But corporations and residents may deposit the converted RMB in the bank where RMB is converted. (Actually, they may come to a certain bank to convert money because they have deposit in the bank.) As a result, major banks hold much more base currency than emerging ones. In other words, through this channel, big banks get bigger and monopolize pricing emerge in the money market.

Different Influences on Interest Rate

In injecting the same amount of base currency, the injection in the form of fund outstanding for foreign exchange will lead to higher interest rate compared to open-market operation. Open-market operation has direct and decisive influence on interest rate, while the influence from the other

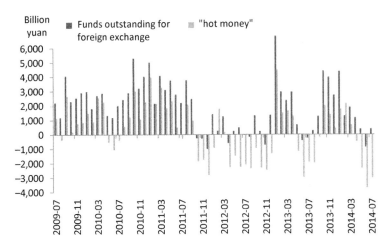

Figure 1.18   "Hot money" is the major form of inflow when funds outstanding for foreign exchange cycle remain positive. (Citation: WIND)

model depends on the risk preference of base currency holders, which is indirect and uncertain. According to the estimated scale of "hot money" based on "funds outstanding for foreign exchange cycle-trade balance-FDI," when funds outstanding for foreign exchange cycle flow in, additional "hot money" inflow accounts for over 50% of China's funds outstanding for foreign exchange cycle. The high risk of "hot money" determined that it does not circulate in money market or even banks; instead, it is directly invested in financial assets, which have a much higher interest rate than bank deposit or money market. In comparison, open-market operation targets banks and other major financial institutions, directly influencing the interest rate of money market. Meanwhile, banks are the least risky in the market. Therefore, with certain amount of base money, open-market operation is more effective in lowering money market interest rate, whereas the other model has little effect.

In retrospection of China's scale and interest rate of funds outstanding for foreign exchange cycle, we may find that more inflow of this fund resulted in higher interest rate, and vice versa. This is contrary to our common understanding. A typical example is, during the fourth quarter of 2013, when funds outstanding for foreign exchange cycle were transacted in bulk, the interest rate of money market skyrocketed. In 2014, when the

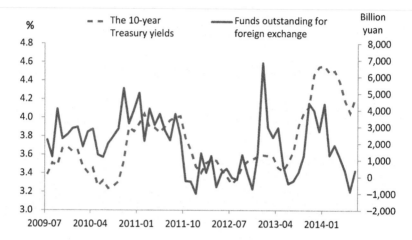

Figure 1.19 Contrary to our common understanding, more funds outstanding for foreign exchange lead to higher exchange rate in most cases. (Citation: WIND).

funds outstanding for foreign exchange cycle was close to nil and the increased rate of base currency balance declined significantly, the interest rate of money market remained low and the yield of bond market plummeted. All these proved that in injecting base currency, more funds outstanding for foreign exchange cycle resulted in higher interest rate.

Different ways of injecting base currency have huge impact on the central bank's turn from quantity regulation to price regulation, as well as interest rate liberalization. When open-market operation is the dominant model, the central bank's interest rate regulation has a clear direction: "central bank → interest rate of money market → other interest rates → real economy." One important precondition is the central bank's direct control over interest rate. When the injection of funds outstanding for foreign exchange cycle is the main channel, the central bank does not control the interest rate directly. The above mechanism fails to function. The conduction mechanism of monetary policy is severely interfered by base currency holders' behavior preferences. Banks mainly hold base currency in forms of residential or corporate deposit. Hence, it is reasonable for the central bank to determine deposit interest rate to adjust the cost of the banking industry; otherwise the central bank will lose the means to regulate the overall interest rate. However, this regulative measure is only an administrative intervention and not a market adjustment. Therefore, when the injection of funds outstanding for foreign exchange cycle is the main channel, the basis for the central bank to regulate price, or conduction path of interest rate does not exist; and the precondition for interest rate liberalization, or liberalizing deposit interest rate is not realistic. In conclusion, the ways of injecting base currency are of vital importance for the transformation of the central bank's policy framework.

Chapter Two

Restructuring Government–Market Relation — Superstructuralism

Government–market relation is essential to the deepening of economic system reform. The 14th National Congress of the CPC announced the decision of "letting the market play a basic role in allocating resources under socialist state macro control." After that, documents of several important meetings all kept this rhetoric. In "Decision of the CCCPC on Some Major Issues Concerning Comprehensively Deepening the Reform" published after the 3rd Plenary Session of the 18th CPC Central Committee, the notion of "market playing a decisive role in resource allocation" was brought up for the first time. The change from "basic" to "decisive" is a fundamental one.

The focus of this chapter is whether or not comprehensive marketization is the best option. In Section one, I point out that the market is not omnipotent and that comprehensive marketization is not advisable due to problems existing in both dimensions of time and space. In Section two, I review old and new structuralism in development economics as well as structural monetary policies of Europe and the US, providing theoretical support and practical experience for structural policies. In Section three, I raise the notion of "superstructuralism," the core of which lies in identifying the boundary between the government and the market, ensuring that government and market each plays its role, and in adopting structural marketization policies.

41

SECTION ONE: COMPREHENSIVE MARKETIZATION IS NOT THE BEST OPTION

As the government becomes clear about "letting the market play a decisive role in allocating resources," domestic support for comprehensive marketization is gradually gaining the upper hand. This is a step forward compared to the previous inflation of government authority. Yet I have harbored many doubts about whether China currently should really pursue comprehensive marketization. These concerns can be divided into two types: those related to the dimension of space and those related to the dimension of time. The former type points to the fact that marketization is not omnipotent and that market does have its limitations, which means it is only natural that marketization also has boundaries. The latter type of concerns refers to the fact that with many unfinished preparations, conditions for comprehensive marketization are not yet optimum in China, so disordered marketization resulting from reckless implementation could affect the economy.

Dimension of Space

The dimension of space refers to the fact that market's finite nature prevents it from being omnipotent, which is what the concept of "market failure" in economics means. This mainly consists of the following types: imperfect competition, externality, insufficient information, distorted utility and opportunity value and accumulation of currency. These may be elaborated as follows:

Imperfect competition: This means that to some extent monopoly exists in the market, where there is at least one buyer (or seller) strong enough to affect the market price. Labor market, intermediate goods market and imported consumer goods market operating under imperfect competition have weakened the exchange-rate pass-through on prices of China's exported goods. (For example, changes in labor costs would partly resolve the pass-through on costs or even prices of exported goods. Chinese producers need to import a large amount of intermediate goods, which have relatively weak substitutability against domestic ones. So exchange-rate fluctuations have a big impact on intermediate goods, and therefore affect the costs and so partly cancel out initial price changes of Chinese exported goods. Currently, goods imported into China are mainly technology-intensive and capital-intensive ones, which are usually under imperfect competition. Thus, foreign exporters have a relatively strong pricing power, leading to a rather significant responsiveness towards exchange-rate fluctuations.)

Externality: Externality occurs when a party's economic activity affects another party in a way unreflected in market transaction. An externality can be an external cost or an external benefit. The most classic examples of an external cost are pollution and consumption of resources, raw materials and public goods caused by manufacturing (e.g., the wearing of roads and bridges due to overload). External benefits can be found in basic industries, urban public infrastructure development and other quasi-public welfare industries.

Insufficient information: Market participants do not have all the knowledge of a certain economic environment, therefore those who have relatively sufficient information tend to be in a favorable position. In terms of real estate loans, for example, efficiency of loan allocation is lowered by insufficient information of banks. Because of information insufficiency, investors demand higher returns in exchange for credit risk of corporate bonds, pushing up the credit spread of bond issuers. Similarly, in tax collection, it happens that tax collected is less than tax evaded. In the insurance industry in particular, information insufficiency is likely to cause adverse selection and moral hazard.

Distorted utility and opportunity value: To allocate resources, the market depends on utility, which may be distorted. For example, infrastructure development provides low utility for all market participants, but government-led infrastructure development does have long-term utility. There could also be opportunity value, i.e., although there is no short-term return, there is potential return in the future. For example, the timing of investment creates an opportunity cost of time for an investment, but high returns might be yielded.

Accumulation of currency: In a market economy, a rich–poor gap will emerge. The rich will accumulate money, slowing down currency circulation and therefore distorting monetary policy control. "Accumulation of currency" refers to the phenomenon in which currency stops being the intermediary in the exchange of goods and so cannot serve as a medium of exchange. Types of currency accumulation include funds which banks are unable to lend out, idle funds in the security market, cash in hand of individuals or institutions, deposits, in effect irretrievable bad loans, foreign balance outside of domestic financial system, currencies used for payments in neighboring countries and currencies stored in fixed assets with low liquidity such as infrastructure or housing (e.g., house prices obviously entail accumulation of currency), etc.

Dimension of Time

The dimension of time refers to the fact that China does not have the prerequisites for comprehensive marketization, that reckless marketization would result in deviation of plan, causing problems such as failure of macro control, soaring financial risks and deteriorating business environment for small and micro enterprises.

Failure of macro control: China is still in a transformation period. The function and position of the state's macro control of this country now are more important whether compared to other countries or to China in the past. Economic transformation cannot be conducted by the market spontaneously. Rather, it requires adequate state intervention in aspects such as institutions. The structural monetary policies implemented by the central government in 2014 provide favorable conditions for the development of small and micro enterprises. This is what is needed in the initial period of transformation.

Soaring financial risks: Marketization needs to be safeguarded by supervisory policies. Otherwise, it could lead to distortions in financial innovation, thus amplifying risks in the financial system. Judging by history, interest rate marketization is bound to increase the risk appetite of financial institutions, which will amplify financial risks. Supervision of margin trading and short selling introduced in early 2015 can prove that a prerequisite for the establishment of a large, integrated financial market is integrated or, at least, coordinated supervisory policy, otherwise money is bound to rush into high-risk areas.

Deteriorating business environment for small and micro enterprises: Small and micro enterprises are at a natural disadvantage in the market. Comprehensive marketization would mean that large enterprises could use various methods to suppress small and micro enterprises, e.g., by waging a price war. The main significance of small and micro enterprises is employment. If large enterprises becoming monopolies would cause widespread unemployment, employment as a major objective of macro control would be hard to realize. How could we curb excess competition while increasing market efficiency through competition? This would require further analysis of institutional design.

The chapter "How Far Are We from Interest Rate Marketization" will provide more elaborated discussions on interest rate marketization. We will see that China still has a long way to go in terms of infrastructure development in the financial sector.

SECTION TWO: THEORY AND PRACTICE OF STRUCTURAL POLICIES

I believe that structural marketization is the best approach for China's market-based reform. A review of economic history helps to shed light on structural policies in two aspects: structuralism in development economics and structural monetary policies adopted by the US and EU central banks. These two aspects will be discussed in this section, which I hope can serve as a reference as China tries to address its structural concerns.

Old and New Structuralism

Structuralism in development economics is divided into the old and the new. It is generally believed that old structuralism originated with Rosenstein Rodan (1943) and became popular after World War II, while new structuralism was put forward in 2009 by Justin Yifu Lin, the then Chief Economist of World Bank. Based on structural differences between developing and developed countries, both theories acknowledge the government's leading role in a country's progress towards a higher development level. But they disagree on what goal the government should achieve and through what intervention measures.

Old structuralism argues, "industrialization could not take place spontaneously in developing countries because of structural rigidities and co-ordination problems." As Lin points out, "the old structural economics advocates development policies that go against an economy's comparative advantage and advise governments in developing countries to develop advanced capital-intensive industries through direct administrative measures and price distortions." Old structural economics assumes that "the market failures that make the development of capital-intensive industries difficult in developing countries are exogenously determined by distorted price signals due to the existence of monopolies, labor's perverse response to price signals, and/or the immobility of factors." It also assumes a binary classification of countries, i.e., "low-income, periphery countries" versus "high-income, core countries," and hence a dichotomy to describe the differences between developed and developing countries.

By contrast, Lin's new structuralism is based on the following ideas. First, an economy's endowments and its endowment structure (defined as the relative abundance of labor and skills, capital, and natural resources) are given at any specific level of development and change over time. As a result, the optimal industrial structure also varies with development levels. Second, "each development level is a point along the continuum from a low-income agrarian economy to a high-income industrialized economy, not a dichotomy of two economic development levels ('poor' versus 'rich' or 'developing' versus 'industrialized')." Third, at each given development level, "the market is the basic mechanism for effective resource allocation." "Economic development as a dynamic process entails industrial diversification and upgrading and corresponding improvements in infrastructure at each level."

On fiscal policies, old structuralists hold that the government should control natural monopolies through state-owned enterprises, revenues from which should be invested in non-resource sectors or such social projects as education and public health. New structuralists recommend, "an appropriate share of revenues from resource commodities be invested in human capital, infrastructure and social capital." They also advocate a counter-cyclical policy, encouraging governments to invest in infrastructure during economic recessions.

On monetary policy, old structural economics suggests that autonomy should not be granted to central banks and monetary policy should be "directed at influencing interest rates and credit allocation." New structural economics advocates the use of interest rate policy as a counter-cyclical tool to encourage infrastructure and industrial upgrading investments during recessions.

In particular, Lin provides a six-step procedure of "growth identification and facilitation" for developing countries. "Step 1: Governments should select dynamically growing countries with a similar endowment structure and with about 100% higher per capita income than their own average. They must then identify tradable industries that have grown well in those countries for the previous 20 years. Step 2: If some private domestic firms are already present in those industries, they should identify constraints to technological upgrading or further firm entry, and take action to remove such constraints. Step 3: In industries where no domestic firms are present, policy-makers may try to attract foreign direct investment (FDI) from countries listed in step 1, or organize new firm-incubation programs. Step 4: In addition to the industries identified in step 1, the government should also pay attention to spontaneous self-discovery by private enterprises and support the scaling up of the successful private innovations in new industries. Step 5: In countries with poor infrastructure and a bad business environment, special economic zones or industrial parks may be used to overcome barriers to firm entry and FDI and encourage the formation of industrial clusters. Step 6: The government should be willing to compensate pioneer firms in the industries identified above with tax incentives for a limited period, co-financing for investments, or access to foreign exchange."

In my opinion, despite the emphasis on the market's role in facilitating industrial development, new structuralism does not deviate from Keynesianism. In fact, it is the application of comparative advantage in Keynesianism: the government, instead of the market, plays the leading role and determines a country's industrial structure and development pattern.

Structural Monetary Policy in the US and EU

Since 2008, the EU and the US have adopted multiple complex monetary policies. Especially after the failure of money supply loosening and the emergence of liquidity trap, structural monetary policies have become a common choice in the western world. These policies fall into two categories: one is to adjust the term structure of interest rate; the other is to provide targeted policy support for certain sectors.

Quantitative easing (QE) is a typical policy to lower certain interest rates. QE is an intervention measure adopted by the central bank to increase monetary base and inject liquidity into the market through purchase of government bonds and other middle- and long-term bonds. Unlike interest rates, QE is not a standard instrument. A typical example of QE can be found in Japan during 2001–2006 when the central bank reduced policy interest rates to zero and bought a certain amount of middle- and long-term government bonds to fight deflation. From 2008 to 2013, the US carried out three rounds of QE and "operation twist." These policies were meant to increase money supply and lower middle- and long-term interest rates through expanding the central bank's balance sheet, which hopefully will address deflation, recover credit and prevent the worsening of economy.

A typical example of monetary policy which provides targeted support for certain sectors is the targeted long-term refinancing operations (TLTROs) launched by the European Central Bank in June 2014 to support bank lending to households and non-financial corporations. With the longest maturity of four years, the TLTROs are tied to loans to euro-area non-financial private sectors (excluding loans to households for house purchase) and are estimated to involve up to 1 trillion euros. TLTROs are carried out in two phases: In the first phase, through two operations in September and December 2014, banks were able to borrow an amount equivalent to up to 7% of their loans to euro-area non-financial private sectors, or 400 billion euros as estimated; in the second phase, through six quarterly operations from March 2015 to June 2016, banks could get additional borrowing allowance which was limited to three times the difference between the net lending to euro-area non-financial private sectors and the benchmark. The market generally applauds the central bank's effort to link liquidity injection with banks' lending, believing that it will greatly improve the financing environment for small- and medium-sized companies. However, despite the central bank's great efforts, these structural monetary policies did not achieve the goal of "adjusting the structure." One reason is the blocked transmission mechanism of monetary policy: banks are reluctant to lend, hence a great amount of money held up within banks.

The crux of achieving "targeted operation" through structural monetary policy is banks lending to certain sectors as the central bank wishes. During the economic crisis, however, structural monetary policy may be helpful in forming a mechanism that encourages banks to lend, but is unable to address banks' concerns. As the sluggish economy makes companies' life harder, big blue-chip companies are less willing to invest and small- and medium-sized companies are more likely to be exposed to credit risks. To control risks, banks tend to tighten up their credit, which, however, is inconsistent with the central bank's intention of credit easing. If banks take measures otherwise, for example, lending more to small- and medium-sized companies, they may face higher risks posed by more bad debts and lower capital adequacy ratio.

In fact, banks' applications in the first round of TLTRO were less than expected. This indicated euro-area banks' prudence. As the EU-wide bank stress testing was in October and coming near, it was understandable that banks were unwilling to lend to small- and medium-sized companies for fear of widening capital gap. China has seen a rapid growth in non-performing loans in recent years. As a result, Chinese commercial banks' reluctance to lend may also undermine the effectiveness of structural monetary policy.

SECTION THREE: CHINESE CHARACTERISTICS AND SUPERSTRUCTURALISM

In Davos of 2015, Premier Li Keqiang raised the concept of "twin engines" for the first time: "Chinese will give full play to 'the two hands' of government and market to form the 'twin engines'. On the one hand, we will cultivate the new engine by letting the market play a decisive role in resource allocation; on the other hand, we will reform and upgrade the traditional engine by letting the government better play its role."

Regarding Premier Li's new interpretation of the relationship between the market and the government, I could not agree more. This interpretation basically conforms to "the superstructuralism" that I came up with, which has the following four core points:

- The absolute majority of departments should be completely liberalized: the boundary between the government and the market should be clearly defined; fiscal and taxation institutional reform should be pushed forward to remove the intervention of soft budget constraint in the marketization endeavor. The PPP mode should be promoted; pricing should be market-based; small and micro-sized enterprises can be the starting point for creating a market environment of perfect competition.
- The government should dominate areas where it enjoys comparative advantages and the market fails, such as areas that heavily rely on science and technology and capital, for example, high-speed railway, nuclear power and aviation, and public services whose investment return rate is low.
- A differentiated development strategy should be adopted for regions at different development stages. A typical example is East China and West China. Their development driving forces are different. There still exists a strong need and huge potential to develop infrastructure in West China.
- Structural monetary policies should be implemented. According to the theory of the second best, non-market distortion can be likewise redressed with non-market measures to realize Pareto optimum under the constraints imposed by non-market departments.

Superstructuralism is significantly different from the new structuralism, the old structuralism and the structural monetary policies of the US and Europe. Both the new structuralism and the old structuralism stress industrial restructuring through government-led investment and put monetary policies at a subordinate status as only aggregate policies. Superstructuralism holds that the government–market relationship should be restructured; the decisive role of the market must be established and the government's role lies in redressing market failures rather than interfering in the market; fiscal policies should give way to monetary policies and monetary policies and other supporting measures should demonstrate structural features. The difference between superstructuralism and structural monetary policies is: the latter was set against the background of liquidity trap and the short-term interest rate was close to zero and it cooperated with and complemented the aggregate easing monetary policies; the former is structural monetary policies adopted while the aggregate policies remain basically unchanged.

Regarding monetary policies, the monetary policy framework changed; the meaning of the central bank's monetary policy goals was adjusted; innovative monetary policy tools emerged, structural monetary policy became the New Normal and supporting measures including regulation were strengthened.

Specifically speaking, of the central bank's ultimate goals, growth, inflation employment goals are all of structural significance. The one on financial systemic risk has structural features. The growth goal not only involves aggregate growth, but also specifically requires promoting the development of agriculture, farmers and rural areas, small and micro-sized enterprises, science and technology, the new type of urbanization and other relevant areas. The inflation goal gradually shifts to focus on core CPI. Since 2013, the National Bureau of Statistics started to publish the core CPI and the CPI excluding fresh vegetables and fruits and traced the latter back to 2005. This may provide a new "anchor" for inflation regulation and control. Employment is increasingly important, and its connection with growth has been weakened. This is closely related to the share of service in GDP. Financial systemic risk started to become one of the central bank's ultimate goals. Please refer to the section on "The Amended Taylor Rule" in this chapter for more detailed information.

• Monetary policy tools are innovated to form many kinds of structural tools, such as targeted reserve requirement ratio cuts, targeted interest cuts, targeted re-discount and re-lending, pledged supplementary lending (PSL) and so on. Through controlling the flow of capital, targeted monetary policy tools change the capital distribution structure so as to influence the structural adjustment. This will be elaborated on in the chapter on monetary policy tools.

• New changes happen to the transmission mechanism. The central bank's issuance of base money starts to have implications for prices and it

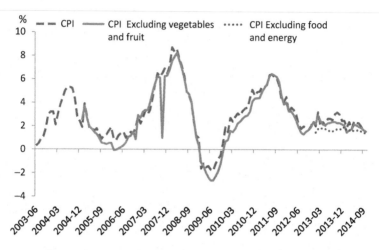

Figure 2.1   There are currently three CPI indexes in China.

starts to shift away from quantity-based regulation to price-based regulation. The issuance of base money used to be passive in the form of funds outstanding for foreign exchange. Under the mechanism of foreign exchange settlement and sale, this is equivalent to the central bank directly issuing money to residents or enterprises, not conveying price signal to commercial banks. The new tool is the central bank providing commercial banks with base money, which can be seen as a price signal and thus provide a channel for price regulation. In the future, we will see the formation of a price-based regulation system featuring the interaction of many kinds of policy rates such as open market operation interest rate, interest on excess reserves, standing lending facility operational rate and pledged supplementary lending rate.

• This structural monetary policy is under aggregate constraint. Compared with the structural monetary policies of the US and Europe, the biggest difference of those of China is the aggregate constraint. The reasons for the overall monetary easing in the US and Europe include the complete burst of the real estate bubbles, low inflation or even deflation, and banks' shrinking appetite for risks leading to huge amount of capital sitting in the interbank market. Thus, the European central bank had to resort to negative interest rate to compel banks to loan óut the money that they deposit in the central bank and the money multiplier dropped to the lowest in history. China's situation is hugely different from that of the United States. First, China's real estate enters the equilibrium range and the bubbles do not burst. If the central bank issues excessive money while the investment channels are limited, there exists the risk that housing price will rise again. Second, historical experience shows that too much liquidity released by the central bank will surely be followed by high inflation, which will jeopardize the hard-won low inflation in China. Third, Chinese financial institutions' preference for risks remains fairly high. From 2012 to 2013, non-standard bond assets ("the non-standard") were excessive in the market. In 2014, the non-standard that falls into the category of commercial paper still enjoyed quite a huge market. At last, China's money multiplier keeps increasing, and in June 2014, it approached the highest level since 2008. This determines that the central bank cannot implement the aggregate easing policy. The structural monetary policy under aggregate constraint is unique to China. It is more difficult to regulate than the structural monetary policy under aggregate easing. This is one reason why I name it "the superstructuralism."

It targets structural market failure but is different from traditional industrial policies. China's market failure is different from that proposed by the new structuralism and the old structuralism. What exists in China is not only free market failure but also the absence of conditions for free market. Due to trust funds' obligation to pay the investors in all conditions, soft intervention and bubbles, banks much prefer state-owned enterprises to small and medium-sized enterprises when giving loans. Considering the loan issuers, state-owned enterprises account for a much larger share than private enterprises. This, to a large degree, hampers market-based resource allocation. Such market failure is not the same as that under complete market conditions. In the case of China's market failure, the government should promote the role of the market instead of trying to replace it. Specifically speaking, on the one hand, the government should adopt structural monetary policies to offset the market's aversion to small and micro-sized enterprises and agriculture, the rural areas and farmers. On the other hand, the State Council as a whole should clear away the barriers against marketization. The principle for the country's overall transformation is promoting innovation, the service industry and consumption, which will change the driving force for the economy. This change corresponds to the four stages of national competitive development proposed by Michael Porter. The superstructuralism is essentially different from the new structuralism in that the latter advocates encouraging specific industries through government investment. I believe that the government is unlikely to advocate industrial adjustment after learning lessons from the photovoltaic sector and so on; what is reasonable is allowing free market competition creating a proper environment and favorable conditions.

(d) It implements regulation and other supporting measures for monetary policies and integrates the basic idea of the macroprudential framework. In the wake of the 2008 international financial crisis, macroprudence became the common choice of major central banks to handle financial systemic risks. Although China did not suffer from systemic risks, it pays more and more attention to macroprudence and considers its implementation increasingly necessary. The core of macroprudence lies in responding to the greater financial systemic risks caused by market failure, including large maturity mismatch, leverage, ignorance of liquidity management and excessive preference for risks in financial institutions. The money shortage in 2013 and the soaring interest rate of the money market, the bond market and the paper market are closely related to the lack of supervision. The strengthened supervision constituted an important feature of the financial market in 2014. Under structural monetary policies, strengthening supervision is the basic condition for the effective enforcement of monetary policies. In 2014, the focus of both strengthening supervision and encouraging policies was on the same area: rural financial institutions such as rural commercial banks and rural credit cooperatives. On the one hand, the capital flow of these financial institutions is strictly controlled ("The Notice on Strengthening Supervision on the Non-standard Bond Assets Investment Business of Small and Medium-sized Rural Financial Institutions" and "The Notice of the General Office of the CBRC on Strengthening Supervision on the Capital Business of Rural Cooperative Financial Institutions"); on the other hand, low-cost capital is used to encourage credit support for agriculture, rural areas and farmers and small and micro-sized enterprises. Structural regulation policy and structural monetary policy are important features of the superstructuralism.

Chapter Three

A New View of Interest Rate Liberalization

After the "cash crunches" in June 2013, the interest rates in China's money market and bond market have soared to a historical high level. One of the leading explanations at that time was that along with the advancement of interest rate liberalization, the upward trend of interest rates was inevitable. Since then, interest rate liberalization has attracted a lot of attention. In 2014, however, interest rates in money market dropped sharply. If we follow the previous explanation, the big drop in interest rate remains a puzzle. By then, this research area has faded away and interest rate liberalization has become a cliché.

However, there are still a lot of problems and much misunderstanding that need to be solved for interest rate liberalization. For example, is there a link between the mid-2013 rising interest rates and the interest rate liberalization? Does interest rate liberalization necessarily imply a market-determined interest rate? Is removing deposit rate ceiling the final step for interest rate liberalization in China? And what is the next step after interest rate liberalization?

In this chapter, I have come to three conclusions: First, for China, there is still a long way to reach full interest rate liberalization. Second, the major goals of interest rate liberalization are to construct the financial infrastructure and to enhance the money policy transmission mechanism.

Last, the interest rate liberalization does not necessarily lead to a rising interest rate, which depends on the level of financial repression and the changes of real interest rates in other countries.

The structure of this chapter is as follows: Section One gives an overview of the interest rate liberalization, the introduction of interest rate liberalization, the background of China's interest rate liberalization and the changes that have taken place in 2013. Section two elaborates on the monetary policy transmission mechanism after interest rate liberalization and the reasons for why I think there is still a long way to reach full interest rate liberalization in China. Section three lists the three-step framework of interest rate liberalization and introduces the important theory of "The Modified Taylor Rule." Section four presents the condition under which interest rate liberalization will lead to rising rate and predicts the future trend of interest rate in China.

SECTION ONE: WHAT IS INTEREST RATE LIBERALIZATION?

Starting from the "Decision on Reform of the Financial System of the State Council" in 1993, interest rate liberalization has been carried out for more than 20 years. Yet, there is still some misunderstanding regarding interest rate liberalization in the market. For example, until 2013, numerous people believed that interest rate liberalization is directly linked with market-determined interest rates: financial institutions decide the rates based on their capital position and the market trend and the central bank should not interfere with the interest rate market. Their point is wrong since they mistakenly draw an analogy between the interest rate market and the exchange rate market, which are obviously not appropriate. It is true that central banks should stop foreign exchange intervention but it is not the case for interest rate market. Some people would say that it is feasible if the central bank does not decrease the monetary base. However, with the development of economy and the increase of GDP, a larger monetary base is essentially needed. Then without any open market operation to increase the monetary base, the interest rate will rise naturally, even higher than the real economy's equilibrium interest rate. In fact, any action that the central banks take to adjust the amount of monetary base would affect the interest rates. As a result, one can never separate the central bank from the interest rate market.

The interpretation of interest rate liberalization given by the People's Bank of China is as follows: "Interest rate liberalization is essentially a process of market mechanism gradually playing a role in interest rate determination to optimize the capital allocation. Yet interest rate liberalization does not mean interest rate is totally liberated. The central bank can affect the market benchmark interest rates by open market operation in order to further affect the pricing of other financial products." I do generally agree with this point but further explanations are required for demonstrating the role of the central bank after interest rate liberalization and the relationship between interest rate liberalization and regulation.

First, we need to clarify that the interest rate system is multi-level, different kinds of investors participating in different levels. Individuals, corporations and commercial banks are participants for the deposit and loan market while corporations and institutional investors are participants in the corporate bond market. For both markets I mentioned above, the central bank will not and should not interfere with the interest rates directly; it should be determined by market investors' capital supply and demand. Commercial banks and the central bank are major players in the money market. As a major player in money market, the central bank has to involve in deciding the money market interest rates. In other words, it is true that the interest rate liberalization requires market-determined interest rates. It is also true that the central bank is one of market participants now. Thus, the central bank has a great power in influencing market interest rates. In fact, money markets in the US, Europe and other countries are monoplied by their central banks, as well as money market interest rates, for the central banks have the unlimited ability to release and withdraw base money.

Second, interest rate control must be carried out through a market-based way. As mentioned above, the central bank does not directly participate in and intervene with credit market, but it can influence credit market by regulating money market rates. Regarding money market, the central bank can only control interest rates by open market operations, rather than administrative measures. Namely, the central bank decides to increase or decrease the monetary base, influencing the market dynamic of the monetary base, so that the interest rates are decided in a market-oriented way.

Last, the benchmark interest rate should be determined by the central bank, while the credit spread and term spread should be decided by other market participants. From the perspective of interest rate structure, market rate equals the sum of benchmark rate, credit spread and term spread. Among them, the benchmark interest rate is generally the overnight money market rates, which are determined by the central bank (for Europe and the US). The Federal Reserve controls the level of interest rates while the European Central Bank decides the interest rate range. It is generally believed that the credit spread and term spread of the overnight money market rates are zero, since it has the shortest duration and the lowest risk. Other interest rates need to count the credit spread and term spread, which are decided by market participants. Take corporate bonds for example, the credit spread and term spread are determined by the bond maturity and the corporate credit rating, both of which are not controlled by the central bank.

In conclusion, interest rate liberalization refers to the participants of each market determining interest rates in a market-based way. In money market, the central bank, as a major participant, controls the money market rates by open market operations, while other interest rates are decided by the benchmark interest rate, adding the credit spread and term spread, both of which are entirely determined by market.

Why are Not Interest Rates Market-Based under the Old Normal?

According to our analysis above, we cannot solely blame the central bank intervention on deposit and lending rate for non-market-based interest rates.

Firstly, the central bank directly decides the benchmark interest rates (deposit and lending rates), rather than controlling the monetary base. By this administrative intervention, the central bank distorts the interest rate dynamics and ignores the market supply and demand. Since the actual market interest rates are decided by the real money market supply and demand, the actual rates are different from the official target rates, a double-track system of interest rates. Comparatively, in Europe and the US, though the central banks set the benchmark interest rates, they use open market operations to influence the supply of money in the economy to make the actual rate follow their target/official rate. Therefore, the administrative intervention is one of the reasons why China's interest rates are non-market-based.

However, the central bank can also set the target rate close to the market equilibrium interest rate, so that the administrative intervention does not result in a strong financial repression. In Section Four, we will study whether the deposit and lending rates are repressed in China and the future interest rates trend after interest rate liberalization.

Second, under the Old Normal, the deposit and lending rates in China are totally controlled by the central bank, without any risk factors. In Europe and the United States, the spread between the actual overnight rate and the target rate is almost fixed, so we can assume that the prime lending rates is directly controlled by central banks without administrative provisions. However, the lending rates for corporates equal the sum of the prime rate and the relative risk premium. But in China, banks make loans to different corporates at the same official interest rate. The absence of risk factor in pricing methodology is the second feature of Chinese interest rate market before liberalization.

Third, the central bank puts restriction on the source and application of loans. On the one hand, loans are outstripping deposit. Because of the restriction on the loan-to-deposit ratio, the loan size must be less than deposit size, causing a separation between credit market and money market, failure of conduction mechanism between the two markets. On the other hand, the central bank provides actual window guidance to commercial banks on lending issues, including the credit scale and credit industries, even though without any official record. This sort of "unorthodox" guidance from the central bank results in a non-market-based loan system. The administrative intervention on the source and the application of loans is the third feature of the Chinese interest rate market before liberalization.

SECTION TWO: HOW FAR AWAY IS INTEREST RATE LIBERALIZATION FROM US?

According to the government official plan for interest rate liberalization — foreign currency first, then local currency; loan first, then deposit; long-term and large capital first, then short-term and small capital — for now, the control on deposit rate is the only obstacle before interest rate liberalization is completed. In fact, financial products, as the pioneer of interest rate liberalization, reached 14 trillion RMB in 2014. With the addition of two trillion RMB in money market fund, financial products account for 15% of the balance of deposit, more than 30% of the total personal saving. This shows that the role of market forces in small short-term deposit market has been prominently improved and the time to lift the control on deposit rate has come. Zhou Xiaochuan, the governor of the People's Bank of China, said in July 2014 that interest rate liberalization can be realized in two years. So, is interest rate liberalization that close to us?

Zhou has made two important comments on interest rate liberalization in *The Tutorial Book in Decisions of Third Plenary Session of the 18th Central Committee of the Communist Party of China*, as well as in the "Deepening the Reform and Opening up of Financial Industry Comprehensively and Quickening the Improvement of the Financial Market System" published in *People's Daily*.

Zhou emphasized that market forces play a decisive role in the capital allocation. It is necessary to improve the market mechanism and keep government intervention away from the market-determined price. Interest rate and exchange rate, the key price of the factor markets, is the decisive factor in the effective allocation of domestic and international capital. Promoting the exchange rate and interest rate reform gradually can contribute to optimizing the capital allocation efficiency, strengthening market forces' decisive role in factor markets and pushing forward the economic development and restructuring.

He also proposed a three-step approach — in the short term to improve the ability of financial institutions to conduct independent pricing on the assets side, launch lending base interest rates for credit pricing, and promote interbank certificates of deposit on the liabilities side to expand the scope of debt market-based pricing; in the medium term, to improve the market-based interest rate system, enhance the regulation ability of the central bank and optimize the policy transmission mechanism; finally, to realize the full interest rate liberalization and the market-based interest rate regulation mechanism.

Zhou not only pointed out the purpose of interest rate liberalization to improve the efficiency of resource allocation by allowing market forces to play a bigger role in setting factor prices, but also made a three-step plan for interest rate liberalization. We can see that the key and difficult points of interest rate liberalization does not lie in easing the control on deposit interest rates, but in improving the market rate system, the interest rate regulatory framework, the interest rate transmission mechanism and the decisive role of market forces in capital allocation.

After interest rate liberalization, the monetary policy transmission mechanism will be: the central bank regulates the benchmark interest rates, which then influences the financial market, and affects the real economy afterwards. It is very different from that under the old Normal, which works as follows: change of the RMB counterpart of foreign exchange forces the central bank to increase or decrease the monetary base, and then influences the amount of broad money, mainly the credit scale, finally the real economy. The difference in monetary regulation targets and financing leads to the disparity between the two transmission mechanisms. After the full-reach of interest rate liberalization, we need to re-establish the transmission path since the current situation is not ideal enough.

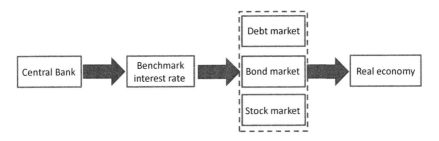

Figure 3.1   The monetary policy transmission mechanism after interest rate liberalization.

Step One: The Central Bank Regulates the Benchmark Interest Rates

The interest rates of money market in China are not controlled by the central bank directly, but decided by financial institutions. This is quite different from the ECB and the Fed who directly control the money market rates because of the different qualitative control and monetary base control measures they take.

Under the Old Normal, monetary base is driven by the fund outstanding for foreign exchange. As mentioned in Chapter One, commercial banks act as a currency exchange agent for individuals, corporates and international investors. As the largest source of funds for commercial banks is deposit, it is more efficient to control deposit rates in order to control the cost.

Under the qualitative measures, the central bank needs to control only the monetary base and the broad money, rather than the money market rates. So the money market is not directly controlled by the central bank, but indirectly affected by the changes of deposit and lending rates.

After 2014, the strength of the fund outstanding for foreign exchange got weakened. The central bank began to adopt new monetary policy instruments to adjust monetary base, such as Medium-term Lending Facility, Pledged Supplementary Lending, and Standing Lending Facility. These new instruments are mainly focused on adjusting the medium-term interest rates, not the short-term money market interest rates. Big hurdles remain for controlling the benchmark interest rates of money market rates, and that is the obstacle to establish the new monetary policy transmission mechanism.

Step Two: The Change of Benchmark Interest Rates Affects Financial Markets

We will mainly focus on analyzing how the benchmark interest rates affect the bond market and the credit market since the range is too large in financial market. These two markets have their own interest rate system, similar to the money market. In general, market rate equals the sum of the benchmark rate, the term spread and the credit spread. However, now for China, how the term spread and credit spread are assessed is problematic.

(a) Maturity mismatch distorts the term spread.

The term structure of interest rates in China is different from other countries: (1) The term spread between overnight rate and one month money market rate is very high. The spread between the overnight rate and the 3-month rate reaches 2%, while that in other countries is nearly zero. (2) The spread between the seven-day rate and the 10-year yield of China Development Bank (CDB) is too low, 1% in China while in the US, it is 2.5% (in order to include the tax factor, we choose the CDB bond since the government bond is tax-free.)

In China, maturity mismatch is very common and it is also an important profit model for most Chinese financial institutions. For example, on the first day, we borrow one billion RMB from money market at the overnight rate, and then buy the one billion CDB bond. On the second day, we pay back the one billion and borrow the same amount from the overnight market again. If we do this repetitively, we can make arbitrage trade and make a profit of the difference between the yield of CDB bond and the cost of overnight rate. As long as we have enough collateral, and the volatility of money market rate keeps stable, we can easily make an arbitrage. As the CDB bond can be considered as a risk-free investment, we only face the liquidity risk of the short-term money market interest rate volatility. Moreover, if the short-term money market rates work as the benchmark interest rates, the liquidity risk will also be eliminated.

If the short-term money market rates is the benchmark, the central bank must release sufficient amount of base money to maintain the target interest rate. In the US, where the money market rates are stable, the riskless arbitrage can be easily made by borrowing short term capital at a fixed rate and conducting the term mismatch, even without liquidity risks. Theoretically, this arbitrage exists until the long-term risk-free bond yield is same as the short-term money market rates. Besides, the high collateral ratio of the risk-free bonds, usually more than 90%, contributes to the high leverage ratio in maturity mismatch.

Generally speaking, I do not believe the maturity mismatch is "bad" for the market; instead, it is an important tool to conduct interest rate transmission from short-term rates to long-term rates. But how to prevent the excessive leverage, which causes the distortion of term structure, is the problem that calls for our attention. Since there is no effective solution to this problem, the central bank now can only adopt medium-term interest rate instruments to avoid the moral hazard caused by the short-term benchmark interest rates.

(b) For credit spread, there are three crucial problems that need to be solved. The first is the lack of effective risk pricing. Investors strongly believe that the trustee will pay the principal and revenue under any circumstances and there will be no default risk in the market. The second is the intervention from companies with soft budget constraints on efficient capital allocation. The last one is the growing asset price bubble which needs to be weakened.

These three obstacles lead to the mismatch between the risk pricing mechanism and the supply and demand mechanism, resulting in inefficient interest rate pricing. For example, companies with soft budget constraints are usually state-owned enterprises or those who are closely related to local governments. By risk pricing, these companies can borrow money at lower rates than others, while by the supply and demand rule, they should be charged by higher rates, because their insensitivity to interest rates and motivation to leverage create their unimaginably high capital demand.

Then, we will exhibit a detailed analysis of three situations where credit spread does not work.

The first is the lack of effective risk pricing. As we know, market rate equals the sum of risk-free rate and the risk premium. The risk-free rate depends on the economy's potential growth rate. Under the monetary policy framework of the benchmark interest rate as the intermediate target, the risk-free rate is controlled by the central bank. Nowadays in China, the risk-free rate is decided by the liquidity in the interbank market with moderate intervention from the central. In this case, the key factor is the effective risk premium, but in China, the lack of effective exit mechanism of enterprises, and the various implicit guarantees result in low default risk. The risk pricing in today's market is based on the uncertainty of the policy, not the default risk. After interest rate liberalization, the real default risk will arise, widening the risk premium significantly. The implicit guarantee and the bailout promises are to lower investors' risk, as well as the financing cost of financial institutions and local governments. The default risk-free market provides products with high yield but low risk, which obviously is inconsistent with the yield curve risk.

The second situation is the intervention from companies with soft budget constraints on efficient capital allocation. We need to distinguish the rate of return and capital efficiency first. In the classical economic model, the market-determined real interest rates help to maximize the capital allocation efficiency. But in China, due to the soft budget constraints, interest rate liberalization does not come along with optimal capital allocation. Zhou interpreted the soft budget constraints as borrowing money without the intention to pay back, in an exclusive interview for the magazine *Caijing* in December 2013. He also mentioned the two forms of soft constraints, one being the borrowing of money through administrative power, and the other, borrowing money regardless of the interest rate, both of which show the impossibility of paying back. The rate of return with soft constraints are usually high, in spite of the low capital efficiency. According to an assessment report from the State Council, investments in infrastructure, overcapacity industries and real estate industry are with low return and long payback period. The first two industries we just mentioned are generally considered as entities with soft budget constraints. If we accomplish the interest rate liberalization without wiping out the soft constraints, though the capital flows freely in the market, the soft constraint entities will offer higher rates since they are insensitive to the high interest rate. Finally, capital will flow to these non-market-oriented entities, increasing the overall rates, same as the result of ineffective risk pricing mechanism. In this way, the soft constraints entities crowd out other companies with urgent capital need and high capital efficiency. In conclusion, the soft constraints prevent the interest rate liberalization from optimizing the capital allocation and further crowd out small business and rural sectors, both of which need capital support most. Several specific measures should be taken: local governments should set up a budget system with hard constraints and control debt scale, such as taking the debt scale into the officials' evaluation system; for overcapacity industries, the central government should carry forward the market-based exit mechanism, encourage merger and acquisition, allow big enterprise to fail, and take social security measures to ensure social stability.

The third problem is the growing asset price bubble. In China, whether there is a real estate bubble is still controversial, but the outrageous prices are indisputable. According to the statistics from Yiju Research Institute, the national residential housing price-to-income ratio is 7.3, while the reasonable ratio suggested by the World Bank is between 3 and 6. We have mentioned when the economy is mainly driven by the infrastructure investment, capitals have largely flowed to the real estate industry, leading to a boom in real estate investment. Meanwhile, speculators drove up the housing price, which in turn led more speculative money to flood in. Between 2012 and 2013, a huge amount of money crowded into the real estate through non-standard financial products. In mid-2013, the real estate development capital increased by more than 30% on a year-on-year basis, while the fixed asset investment growth rate in the corresponding period was only 20%. The land and the property in real estate industry can work as collaterals so under the appreciation expectation, the real estate industry expanded rapidly and became another insensitive sector to interest rates besides the soft constraints. What is more, it is considered as one of the investment fields with low return and long payback period in the assessment report of the State Council. It is important to note that the rate of return for real estate investment is not low, but the capital efficiency is too low to support the long-term economic growth. Mentioned in the last chapter, I believe that the current housing prices have entered the equilibrium interval, but there are still high uncertainties in whether a new round of real estate bubble would arise if the central bank maintains fixed short-term rates. At present, restrictions on house purchasing are lifted in most cities, and there are signs that restrictions on real estate loans will also be lifted. Despite the fact that the real estate industry has not recovered yet, would the price rapidly rise again if local governments lower the housing purchasing cost and lift investment restrictions to facilitate local governments' land finance? It is necessary to treat rigid demand and investment demand differently and take stricter measures to refrain speculation in order to avoid asset price bubble after interest rate liberalization.

In conclusion, these three problems lead to the failure of interest rate liberalization in optimizing capital allocation. Capital flows to the high return sectors, rather than the high efficiency sectors. Theoretically, investors make decision based on the risk and yield expectation. So the more

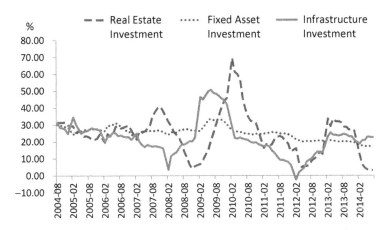

Figure 3.2   The growth rate of infrastructure and real estate investments is higher than that of fixed assets investments. (Citation: WIND)

profitable industry will certainly attract more capital, and the riskier industries will attract less capital, enhancing the capital allocation efficiency. In fact, however, it is not only the companies with high profitability that can offer high interest rates, but also those that are insensitive to interest rates, most of which are with low profitability. In this circumstance, capital will flow to the sectors with high rates and low risk, regardless of the capital efficiency. Therefore, interest rate liberalization is not as easy as lifting the deposit and lending rates control. We need to pay more attention to the real object of interest rate liberalization — efficient allocation of capital — and tackle the three obstacles we presented.

I first proposed this idea at the beginning of 2014, in the reports, "The Substantial Default Alone Cannot Save Bond Market of China," and "The Asymmetric Effects of Interest Rate Liberalization." In June, Sheng Songcheng, the chief of the Financial Survey and Statistics Department of the People's Bank of China, demonstrated a similar theory in the published article "The Relationship between Soft Constraints and High Interest Rates." However, Jing Zhongxia said in "The Bond Yield Curve and the Monetary Policy Transmission" in July that high interest rates represent high risk; the risk-free rates can never be higher than the treasury bonds yield and are not based on the promise to pay back.

Combining these two theories, we can draw the following conclusions. First, economic sectors with soft constraints are like a capital black hole. Their demand for money is infinite so that the collective demand for money of the whole society also becomes infinite, driving up the overall interest rates regarding the classical theory of interest rate. Second, from the perspective of risk pricing, the infinite demand for money means the infinite debt ratio and extremely high risk. So, only the high interest rate can compensate for the high risk. Third, the promises or guarantees of payment partially lower the soft constrained sectors' risk, making them possible to finance. This kind of market failure leads the actual interest rates to be lower than what they should be, crowding out other sectors. Last, risk-free rates are also being driven up, though not because of the soft-constrained sectors but rather the increasing risk preference of the financial institutions. This transmission is realized in two ways. One is through the money market. Sectors with soft constraints borrow money from money market through non-standard financial products, pulling the money market rates up. Since the government bond yield is pegged on the money market rates, an increase in money market rate will result in an increase in the government bond yield. Another way is through the systematic risk way. We have mentioned that the growing risk preference of financial institutions resulted in an increase in systematic risk. The risk-free rate will go up with the systematic risk.

To sum up, I believe that the key of interest rate liberalization is to establish the new monetary policy transmission mechanism. However, the first two steps of this mechanism are defective: the central bank has neither clarified a target of benchmark interest rates, nor has control of the money market rates; maturity mismatch problem exists in term spreads; lack of risk pricing and soft constraints problems cause unfair credit spreads and the asset price bubble has not been completely suppressed.

SECTION THREE: HOW WILL INTEREST RATE LIBERALIZATION BE CARRIED OUT?

In the last section, I presented my view that the key and difficulty of interest rate liberalization has nothing to do with lifting deposit interest rate controls, instead, they are dependent on how the market-based interest rate system is established, how the interest rate regulation and control framework of the central bank are improved, how the interest rate transmission mechanism is rationalized, how the capital allocation efficiency is optimized and how market can play a decisive role in resources allocation. At present, the core problem lies in the absence of established financial infrastructure, which are essential in interest rate liberalization.

From my perspective, I think China has to solve at least the following problems to progress in interest rate liberalization.

First, bridging the currency and credit markets to ensure the effectiveness of benchmark interest rates. I have mentioned that money market and credit market in China are segmented, and this leads to the failure of the transmission of monetary market to credit market. As a result, the central bank of China cannot regulate and control the benchmark rates in a national wide if using overnight money market rates as the benchmark rates, just like other countries do. Therefore, liberating restrictions on loan-to-deposit ratio and changing the deposit-oriented banking operation are essential to improve the effectiveness of benchmark interest rates.

Second, the government needs to figure out how the benchmark interest rates can be set. The main reason why China is unable to implement the model of money market rate working as benchmark rates is because it is extremely difficult to set the level of benchmark rate in the process of interest rate liberalization. If the benchmark rate is low, financial institutions will borrow from interbank market largely, resulting in serious term mismatch and high risk of the financial system. On the other hand, if it is high, financial institutions will shrink their balance sheets, causing serious damage to the real economy. I think in the beginning, the central bank could consider applying the rule of interest rate corridor to set the interest rate benchmark. Considering SLF as interest rate corridor ceiling and the excess deposit reserve rate as floor, we can reach the proper level of benchmark rate through trial and error. The interest rate corridor model does not need the wide and deep Treasury market which is necessary in the open market operation model, besides, it has higher fault-tolerant rate of interest rate range regulation.

Third, the marketization of capital demands. It mainly refers to eliminating soft constraints, improving risk pricing and avoiding asset price bubbles in the process of interest rate liberalization.

Fourth, balancing foreign exchange payments. In the past, the central bank used foreign exchange purchase as an important mean to keep the balance of payments, causing the foreign exchange to be the channel of releasing base money. In the first chapter, I emphasized the weakness of this channel. In this way, the release of base money does not correspond to the short-term supply and demand of banks, and cannot affect the pricing of benchmark rates. Under the interest rate corridor model, the overnight interest rates are decided on the price of the central bank releasing overnight base money. So we have to change the model of foreign exchange driving monetary base. The new problem we will face is the use of foreign exchange deposit. After the RMB exchange rate entering the equilibrium interval, how to take good advantage of the increasing foreign exchange will become the urgent problem of commercial banks. I believe that pushing banks to go global and expanding international financial business is the only choice of China's large commercial banks.

Fifth, establishing medium-term interest rates regulation framework. The defect of interest rate corridor is that the central bank cannot control the medium-term interest rates. That is why Europe adopts regular refinancing operations as supplements. The PSL and re-lending have similar significance. However, as the quantity and price are designated by the central bank, instead of market bidding, the PSL and re-lending are still far away from being the market-based monetary policy instruments.

Sixth, specifying the connection between the short-term and medium-term interest rates. In the US, since the central bank directly controls the overnight rates, financial institutions can receive funding at a fixed rate every day and this leads to same money market rates during each term within a year. However in China, the difference between the overnight rate and the 3-month rates is significant. Whether the spreads still exist if the central bank regulates short-term and medium-term interest rates at the same time is an issue required to be further discussed.

Next, I will divide interest rate liberalization into three stages. The early stage of interest rate liberalization refers to the period when the financial market adopts separate operation and regulation segmentation, the money market has single function, the deposit and loan rates are strictly controlled and the central bank conducted macro regulation in quantity rule. In the medium stage, we should focus on the improvement of regulation framework, the restructuring of market system, the construction of financial infrastructure and the start of macro regulation in price rule. Furthermore, the regulation framework, market system and financial infrastructure should be completed in the last period, and the market will play a decisive role in capital allocation at that time.

The Early Stage of Interest Rate Liberalization

As mentioned before, the early stage of interest rate liberalization refers to the period when the financial markets adopt separate operation and regulation segmentation, money market has single function, deposit and loan rates are strictly controlled and the central bank conducted macro regulation in quantity rule. The corresponding time-point is before 2012.

Separate operation and regulation segmentation. In 1992, the Securities Commission of the State Council and the Securities Regulatory Commission were established, responsible for regulation of stock issuance, while the People's Bank of China still supervised bonds and funds. This marked the beginning of China's separated regulation system. At the end of 1993, the issuance of "Decision on Financial System Reform" laid the basis of separated regulation. Thereafter, four laws and a decision, Law of the People's Bank of China, Commercial Bank Law, Insurance Law, Negotiable Instruments Law and Decision on Financial Crime Punishment, established the separate operation pattern of the financial system in China. This pattern is vulnerable to regulatory vacuum and regulatory arbitrage, as paternalism leads to unequal standards of regulation and difficult coordination of monetary policy and financial regulation causes moral hazard. We will further discuss about these afore-mentioned issues in Chapter Seven.

Monotonous function of money market. In the early stage of interest rate liberalization, due to the separate operation and regulation segmentation, money market was limited to interbank market, as a way to adjust the temporary excess or shortage of cash. Thereafter, funds, the participation of insurance companies and securities companies gradually expanded the money market. But, this was still not the main channel of financing for financial institutions. After 2012, the emergence of non-standard financial products linked money market with trust companies and subsidiary of funds, resulting in a unified monetary market and the substantial mixed operation of financial industry.

Regulation on deposit and loan interest rates. Loosening control on deposit and loan rates is one of the most important features of interest rate liberalization. The central bank deregulated the loan rates in 2013, but the deposit rates were still under stringent restriction. The deposit and loan rate control played a crucial role in China's economic development before 2000. The heavy industrialization in China called for low-cost capital, while the deposit and loan rate control was just the way to offer that. Since 2002, China has switched to export-oriented economy after joining the WTO, largely benefiting from the previous heavy industrialization. From a historical perspective, the central bank's operation of raising or lowering interest rates has a direct impact on interbank money market. This is mainly because under the deposit and loan rate control, the asset revenue and liability cost of banks are limited and the money market, as an important financing way, must be greatly affected.

Under central bank's intervention on currency quantity, market interest rates are supposed to reflect the market demands for capitals. In the situation of growing economy and rising inflation, the monetary demand increases and if the central bank keeps money supply unchanged, the market interest will rise, in accordance with the traditional Taylor rule. According to the empirical formula of the People's Bank of China, money supply growth rate should equal the sum of GDP growth rate, inflation rate and additional two or three percentage point. So when GDP and inflation increase, the money supply grows along with the demand, and the market interest rates depend on the relative growth of supply and demand. In theory, there is a linear relationship between regulation in quantity and price. Except the special or non-linear period such as liquidity trap, the central bank is able to achieve the ideal goal by adjusting money supply.

The Medium Stage of Interest Rate Liberalization

In the process of interest rate liberalization, intensifying competition is common in the banking industry, resulting in improving risk appetite and increasing systematic risk. I think this is the reason for rising interest rates in China. As mentioned in the last section, the transmission can be realized in two ways: one is the money market way and the other is the systematic risk way. Represented by non-standard financial products, financial innovation achieved rapid development between 2012 and 2013. What is more, due to the lag and absence of regulation, regulatory arbitrage and regulatory vacuum provide financial institutions with the best chance to lift risk appetite, which reached the peak in 2013. Therefore, risk appetite of financial institutions will not keep growing and therefore the high interest rate at the end of 2013 represents the peak.

Further analyses suggest that the factors behind the phenomenon in 2013 were complicated. First, under interest rate liberalization, mixed operation sprang up, limits on capital flow were pushed through and the three obstacles, soft constraints, lack of risk pricing, and assets price bubble, appeared together. Thus, the money supply, determined by the central bank on the basis of GDP and inflation, could not meet the real money demand of financial institutions, leading to the rising interest rates. Second, mixed operation was prevalent in financial industry, while the regulation was still segmented. Even though the central bank knew the problem was growing systematic risk, it did not have the authority to execute regulatory measures. Third, systematic risk of the financial industry can be measured by multiplying the risk level of financial products by the leverage ratio of financial institutions. The risk level of financial products depends on regulation, while the leverage ratio is related to money market rates. It may be the central bank's intention to maintain high interest rates and enlarge the volatility of money market in order to lower systematic risk. Fourth, despite the great impact on bonds, money market rates have so little influence on credit market that the central bank has a high tolerance for soaring money market rates.

In order to solve these four problems, I think the main task for medium stage of interest rate liberalization should be the improvement of regulation framework, the restructuring of market system, and construction of financial infrastructure. The improvement of the regulation framework refers to adopting unified and macroprudential regulation in response to the mixed operation and growing systematic risk. Market system restructuring means removing the three obstacles, soft constraints, lack of risk pricing, and assets price bubble. And the construction of financial infrastructure focuses on the establishment of deposit insurance system.

a. *The improvement of the regulation framework*

The central bank introduced macroprudential practice of other central banks in the report of monetary policy implementation in the 2nd quarter of 2013. In the reform of international financial management, the United States strengthened the regulation of the FED on systemically important financial institutions. The British government authorized Bank of England to be responsible for macroprudential regulation and transferred the regulation power from the Financial Services Authority to the central bank. The European government established a European Systemic Risk Board (ESRB) and proposed to set a European Banking Union. In May 2013, the European Parliament passed the Single Supervisory Mechanism (SSM) Act, giving the European central bank the right to supervise large banks directly and to have a say on the supervision of other banks. Besides, the European central bank can take advantage of all the macroprudential measures given by law, including counter-cyclical capital buffer, capital requirements on systemically important institutions and liquidity requirements, etc.

Based on my conjecture that time, the statements in the report indicated that the central bank of China also hoped to gain the regulatory power, and this was proved by what happened later. On August 15, 2013, the State Council agreed to set up the financial regulation coordination inter-ministerial joint conference system, a breakthrough of macroprudential regulation framework in China. In December 2013, the State Council promulgated relevant regulations, establishing the basis of the central bank leading regulation framework and the unified supervision system. According to these regulations, the central bank is responsible for the basic statistical framework, the summary of social financing and the regulations on business beyond the traditional separate operation, especially the shadow banking business. In May 2014, the leading regulation authority of interbank business was changed to the central bank. And in August 2014, the central bank conducted a specific inspection covering all the financial institutions in the banking industry. This series of policies shows that the macroprudential regulation framework and the unified supervision system are basically established.

b. *The restructuring of market system*

The restructuring of market system intends to remove three barriers: lack of risk pricing, soft constraints and real estate bubble.

Breaking down the lack of risk pricing step by step. As mentioned before, the lack of risk pricing is essentially caused by the implicit guarantees of financial institutions or local governments, in the hope of lowering investors' risk, reducing financing cost and therefore raising credit leverage. This provides investors with the high-yield-low-risk products, whose essence is the distortion of the risk-yield rule. Along with the advancement of interest rate liberalization, the problem of imbalance between profit marketization and lack of risk marketization turned much more serious. The high-yield-low-risk products gradually crowd out the financing of normal real economy and cause the soaring social financing cost. At the national level, bankruptcy of corporations and financial institutions was allowed in the policy. Since 2014, the emergence of a series of defaults and events with high credit risk shows the possibility to break the default risk-free expectation. Further, I believe that the material default will occur in private-owned enterprises first, then state-owned ones, in fringe industries first, then core industries, in small businesses first, then big ones, eventually in all types of corporations.

Strengthening the soft constraints. The Chinese soft constraint mainly refers to local governments and state-owned enterprises. After 2012, under severe overcapacity, private-owned enterprises tried to deleverage while state-owned ones kept raising their leverage. Why did the state-owned enterprises, with lower profitability, keep leveraging, exactly in contrast to private-owned ones? The first reason is that those large default risk-free enterprises are more attracted to investors. Second, the insensitivity of state-owned companies to interest rates supports their higher financing cost. To solve soft constraints, different measures should be taken for local governments and state-owned enterprises. For state-owned enterprises, we should promote enterprises marketization in the state-owned enterprises reform, draw a strict boundary between enterprise and government and allow proper default events to correct market expectations. For local governments, the first measure is to limit the financing scale and interest rate. As governments should not be one of the market participants, administrative regulation on them is appropriate. Second, we can draw experiences from the dealings with municipal bond, require local governments to publish their balance sheet and release open data of financial revenues and expenditures, and to improve the local government rating system. The National Development and Reform Commission (NDRC) showed determination to regulate government's financing system and to phase out opaque government financing vehicles, also identified the creation of a municipal bond market in an important document on May 20, 2014. A day after, the State Council approved of 10 local governments, Shanghai, Zhejiang, Guangdong, Shenzhen, Jiangsu, Shandong, Beijing, Qingdao, Ningxia, and Jiangxi, to issue and repay bonds on their own. Though progress has been made to remove soft constraints, serious problems still exist in practice. The pilot local government bonds were issued at a low interest rate, even lower than the bonds issued by the State Council and the Treasury bonds. For example, the rate of government bonds of Shandong province issued in July 2014 was 20 basis points lower than the Treasury bond rate. It forced governments to intervene in issuance administratively. The rate of Beijing government bonds issued in August was required to be 0–15% higher than the Treasury bond rate. All of these were caused by the close relationship between banks and local governments. In August 2014, the National Budget Law was amended to allow Chinese local governments to borrow debts upon approval of the Chinese cabinet, the State Council and provincial governments shall act on behalf of cities and counties which do need debt financing within the quota. This regulation, as well as the phasing out opaque local government financing vehicles, will help to remove soft constraints.

The third one is the assets price bubble. The real estate issue has been discussed in detail in the "New Normal" section of this book. I do think that the real estate prices have entered the equilibrium interval, removing an obstacle for interest rate liberalization. For now, the lift of restriction on house lending may have great impact on market, and the governments may bail out housing market for their own sake. So we should pay attention to the resurgence of speculative investment and prices bubble in real estate field. To tackle this problem, the government should continue to promote indemnificatory housing, maintain restrictions on second house purchasing in megacities, and keep price stable while ensuring basic demand of residents.

c. *The construction of financial infrastructure*

The construction of financial infrastructure focuses on the establishment of deposit insurance system. Making implicit guarantees explicit, therefore, would help to lower risk appetite, which is positive for the bond market. An implicit guarantee is similar as a full coverage insurance embedded with moral hazards. Implicit guarantees lead to increased risk-taking at banks since the government would not allow such important institutions to fail or default on debt. From the commercial banks' balance sheets, we can see an increase of the maturity mismatch and high-risk interbank business on banks, while pursuing expansion in deposit and liabilities. Making implicit guarantees explicit would push forward the credit guarantee liberalization, cultivating public risk awareness and promoting commercial banks' risk and liquidity management.

The explicit deposit insurance system helps to unify the lender of last resort, deposit insurer and deposit regulator, the allocation and coordination of whose power are the fundamental problem of financial safety. In the United States, the core content of regulatory reform after financial crisis is exactly to strengthen the Fed's control on these three functions. Now in China, these three functions have not been unified. The deposit insurance system, led by the central bank, will greatly strengthen the central bank's regulatory power.

What is more, the deposit insurance system will affect commercial banks management and the interest rate level. The deposit insurance system may have more influence on small and medium-sized banks than that for large state-owned banks. The possible deposit flow from small banks to large ones will force banks to improve risk and liquidity management. This contributes to improving overall management of banking industry and raising the bond demand, which will lower the interest rate.

d. *The adjustment from quantity rule to price rule*

Another feature of this period is that the macroeconomic regulation starts to transit from qualitative control to interest rate control and the money market rates have gradually become the operation target of monetary policy. During the "cash crunches" in June 2013, the central bank provided liquidity support to financial institutions that meet the macroprudential requirements, also required large commercial banks to help to stabilize the market. These measures indicate that central banks are regulating the macro by interest rate control. In late 2013, the time-point of the restart and pause of reverse repurchase showed the rule of interest rate corridor. The central bank will restart reverse repurchase to enlarge money supply when the seven-day interest rate is more than 5% and pause it when that rate is lower than 3.5%. In January 2014, the central bank identified SLF as the interest rate ceiling corridor and recognized the interest rate corridor rule as the model of monetary policy in price rule in China. In March 2014, Ma Jun, chief economist of the central bank's research bureau, proposed in a seminar that China should establish a new regulation framework that is similar to Europe, interest rates as the short-term intermediary target and M3 growth rate as the long-term goal. He also described the detailed roadmap: the first step is to establish the real interest rate corridor without announcing the implicit targeted interest rates; the second step is to narrow the interest rate corridor; finally, to cancel the deposit benchmark interest rate and declare the new regulation framework, SLF as interest rate corridor ceiling and the excess deposit reserve rate as interest rate floor and maintain a narrower interest rate corridor by open market operations. I agree with the reasonable and practical roadmap and according to the central bank's action in 2013, the central bank may have begun to implement this roadmap.

e. *The pros and cons of non-standard credit products*

The emergence of non-standard credit products completely changed the structure of the banking industry and the financial system. From my perspective, the non-standard credit product has four functions. First, it connects the interbank money market and the credit market to expand the amount of capital available for banks. Second, it helps banks to circumvent loan-to-deposit ratio regulation. Third, it circumvents the window

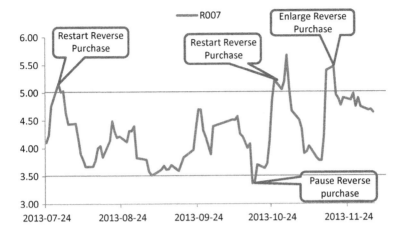

Figure 3.3 Money market interest rate corridor in China. (Citation: WIND)

guidance on loan scale and loan industries to make loans market more market-oriented. Last, it also circumvents the capital requirement under the Basel Agreement. As the non-standard credit products are not included in risk assets, or only 25% is included, while loans are 100% included, it makes great differences in calculating the capital adequacy ratio.

Thus, non-standard credit products have become the magic weapon for banks but a trouble for the central bank.

First, under the old monetary policy framework, the central bank was able to control the credit scale and the loan industries through window guidance, so as to inhibit the black-hole effect in soft constrained industries. Essentially, this is a kind of non-market-oriented regulation on non-market-oriented participants to achieve an equilibrium in the Old Normal. However, the non-standard credit products, beyond the credit scale and industries regulation, leads the capital supply to be market-oriented, contrary to the soft constraints in capital demand. The limited capital supply and the unlimited capital demand result in the soaring interest rates.

Second, the connection between the credit market and the interbank market leads to the substitution effect between interbank borrowing and deposit. As the deposit rate is controlled by the central bank, commercial banks cannot attract more deposit by lifting deposit rate, but borrow money from interbank money market. The high demand in money market had driven the money market rate to soar in the late of 2013. At that time, money market funds sprang up, crowding out the fixed rate deposit. The high money market rate had a strong impact on the stability of banking industry and financial system. The central bank stated in its policy implementation report for the first time that it enforced regulation on the effect that financial innovation has on banking liquidity, which previously were balance of payments and market liquidity.

Third, as the non-standard products circumvent the capital requirement under the Basel Agreement, the overall risk of banking is rising. In order to inhibit the over-leverage in financial institutions, the central bank has no choice but to raise money market rates. It is worth noting that the regulation of the central bank is consistent with that of money markets. Under the framework whose money supply is the operation target, money market is endogenously counter-cyclical. While in those countries where interest rates are the regulating target, this counter-cyclical feature of money market will disappear and the equilibrium target rate plays an important role.

The non-standard credit product, though considered as the negative example of financial innovation, should be critically studied — especially, its impact on interest rate liberalization. There is no dispute about its disadvantages of circumventing regulations. However, I think non-standard credit product has positive influence by breaking the LDR limit, connecting money market and credit market, and circumventing administrative intervention. Thus, I believe that the non-standard product is important financial innovation during the transition from the Old Normal to the New Normal.

The Later Stage of Interest Rate Liberalization

In the later stage, the new regulation framework, the market reconstruction, the financial infrastructure and benchmark interest rate system should be completed, the central bank monetary policies transformed from quantitative-based to price-based, and the market plays a decisive role in capital allocation. As other features have been discussed hereinbefore, we focus on benchmark interest rate system here.

The formation of the benchmark interest rate system is one of the important signs of full interest rate liberalization. Zhou Xiaochuan emphasized that the target direction is to set up an interest rate formation mechanism determined by market supply and demand, and the key task is to improve the market-oriented interest rate system, as well as the interest rate transmission mechanism. According to Zhou, in the near future, the focus should be to perfect the interest rate market-oriented pricing mechanism while improving the independent pricing ability of financial institutions on the assets side, launch lending base interest rates for credit pricing, and promoting interbank certificates of deposit on the liabilities side to expand debt-market-oriented pricing. In the medium term, the focus should be to improve the market-oriented interest rate system, enhance the regulation ability of the central bank and optimize the interest rate transmission mechanism. In my opinion, the final market interest rate system should include benchmark lending rate, Treasury bond yield and SHIBOR, which work respectively as the pricing basis of loans, bonds and short-term financing. For now, benchmark lending rate and the long-term SHIBOR are obviously controlled by large banks, while Treasury bond yield is largely affected by institutional investors. In the later stage of interest rate liberalization, the market interest rate system will get rid of control and manipulation, reflecting the real supply and demand of money, working as the new anchor of monetary policy in price-based regulation.

SECTION FOUR: WILL INTEREST RATE LIBERALIZATION LEAD TO RISING RATE?

In the latter half of the year 2013, the money market rate sharply surged and the bond rate soared. Many institutions attributed it to interest rate liberalization, i.e., the acceleration of interest rate liberalization resulted in the rise of interest rate. However, though interest rate liberalization still continues in 2014, the money market rate declines sharply rather than rises. This raises doubts as to whether interest rate liberalization was the main reason of the high interest rate in the latter half of 2013. Thus, will interest rate liberalization lead to rising interest rate?

In academia, the theory of interest rate liberalization leading to rising interest rate is based on the theory of Financial Repression proposed by McKinnon and Shawn. In practice, Sheng Songcheng, the head of Financial Survey and Statistics Department of PBOC ("Release of Deposit Rate and Upward of Loan Rate") and Zhang Jianhua, the former Head of Research Bureau of PBOC ("Global Experience of Interest Rate Liberalization") have applied data verification. The following part will give a brief introduction about their data verification.

The theory of Financial Repression was proposed by McKinnon and Shawn, specific to the inefficiency of the financial system and the over-supervision on finance in developing countries. They presented that the high nationalization of financial institutions and the low interest rate set by government led to over-demand of social capital. As a result, capital turned into scarce resources and was distributed by the government. In this way, state-owned enterprise, which usually operated inefficiently, got credit loans and hampered the growth of economy.

Sheng Songcheng and Zhang Jianhua tested the interest rate movements in other countries in the process of interest rate liberalization and suggested that the real interest rate rose and the lending and deposit rate spread decreased in most of the countries and regions. The data was acquired in the World Bank's annual statistics of real interest rate in each country, which equals loan rate minus GDP deflator.

I also conducted a research on this, which includes two parts. In the first part, through superposed epoch method, I put the interest rate movements 10 years before and after interest rate liberalization in representative countries on the same graph (with a common event as the zero point of timeline). If interest rate liberalization leading to rising interest rate is a high-probability event, we can obviously see a bunch of curves moving upward over time in the graph. In the second part, I drew the tendency of global interest rate over fifty years, trying to figure out whether there is a consistent tendency of interest rate all over the world and whether the interest rate movement is related to the timing of interest rate liberalization. The data of real loan interest rate was used, acquired from the World Bank, in the study of Sheng Songcheng.

Part One: Analysis on Interest Rate Change Before and After Interest Rate Liberalization by Superposed Epoch Method

I chose nine countries — the UK, France, the US, Japan, Australia, South Korea, India, Thailand and Malaysia — as the study objects. Due to lack of historical data, Germany, Indonesia and other countries were excluded. Superposed epoch method is used to assume the time-point of the same event in different countries to be zero point ($t = 0$), then certain years before and after the event are chosen as the research time interval, and the data of different countries in these years are drawn on the same graph. We can observe whether there is the same feature before and after the event through this graph. In my research, I assumed the timing of lifting controls over wholesale deposits or fixed-term deposit rate as the zero point, 10 years before and after as the time interval. Table 3.1 shows the specific timing of different countries.

My research is different from others in these ways: (1) I focus on the real loan interest rate rather than the nominal rate, because inflation has great impact on the nominal rate while the inflation environments of each country in the process of interest rate liberalization are different; (2) I study about the trend of real loan interest rate, not the fluctuation on some individual time points, which can be easily interfered by inflation abnormal points; (3) I assume the timing of lifting controls on wholesale deposits or fixed-term deposit as the zero point, ten years before and after as the time interval, considering the processes of interest rate liberalization in each country are different and the duration ranges from several years to

Table 3.1   Zero point in superposed epoch method

Nation	Time	Event
The UK	1971	Lifting controls on deposit and lending rate at one time
France	1980	Lifting controls on fixed-term deposit over six months and wholesale deposit more than 500,000 francs
The US	1983	Lifting controls on fixed-term deposit over one month and wholesale deposit more than $ 2,500
Japan	1985	Lifting controls on wholesale deposit more than 10 million yen
Australia	1985	Lifting controls on deposit and lending rate at one time
South Korea (the second time)	1994	Lifting controls on fixed-term deposit over 1 year
India	1997	Lifting controls on fixed-term deposit rate
Thailand	1990	Lifting controls on fixed-term deposit rate
Malaysia (the second time)	1991	Lifting controls on deposit rate

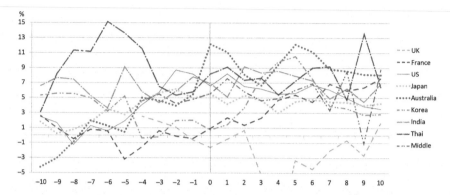

Figure 3.4 The tendency of real loan interest rate before and after liberalization. (Citation: WIND)

decades. For those countries who lift interest rate control gradually, the tendency change of interest rate may be finished at the time of full deposit rate liberalization. That is why I chose one important step in the liberalization process as the zero point, instead of the beginning or ending of interest rate liberalization.

Results are shown in Figure 3.4. We can get the following conclusion: (1) Overall, there is no obvious consistent tendency of real loan interest rate, differences among countries exist. (2) In the process of interest rate liberalization, real loan interest rate kept rising in France and South Korea. (3) Before lifting controls on fixed-term or wholesale deposit, real loan interest rate went upward in the US, Japan, and Australia. (4) Before and after interest rate liberalization, there is no tendency change of real loan interest rate in the UK, India, Thailand, and Malaysia. In conclusion, interest rate liberalization does not necessarily lead to rising interest rate.

Further, in France, South Korea, the US, Japan and Australia, where real interest rate went upward in the process of interest rate liberalization, the real loan rate was near 0% before liberalization, indicating serious financial repression. In India, Thailand, and Malaysia, the real interest rate pivot was about 5% to 7%, without serious financial repression. Thus, we come to the conclusion that serious financial repression is a precondition for interest rate liberalization leading to rising interest rate.

Part Two: Consistent Tendency of Global Interest Rates and the Timing of Interest Rate Liberalization

In the study above, interest rate liberalization leading to rising rates mainly occurred in the 1980s. Is it a coincidence or some kind of inevitable? I further studied about the real interest rate movements in the UK, France, America, Japan, Australia, Korea, India, Malaysia, Thailand and China, and found this is not accidental.

Shown in Figure 3.5, the black solid line represents the median of the real loan rates changing over time and the black dotted line auxiliary presents the trend of global interest rates. The global real interest rates have obvious consistency from 1960s and on (the line as pointed represents China, whose trend independent with the global trend), and can be roughly divided into four stages: in the first stage (1961–1976), global real interest rates moved downward, even become negative; in the second stage (1977–1986), they surged sharply; in the third stage (1987–1997), they kept flat and in the fourth stage (1996–now), the global real interest rates pivot went down slightly and smoothly. In different stages of interest rate liberalization,

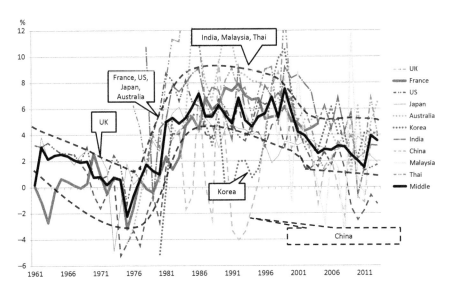

Figure 3.5 The tendency of global real lending rates and the timing of interest rate liberalization. (Citation: WIND)

there are different movements of real interest rate. Interest rate liberalization of the UK occurred in stage one and the real interest rate moved downward along with the global rates; in France, the US, Japan and Australia, i.e., those in stage two, interest rate increased together with the global rates. It is worth noting that though the UK has completed liberalization, its interest rate also rose with the four countries. Thailand, Malaysia and India, in stage three, kept interest rate flat, just like global rates. The interest rate liberalization of South Korea happened in stage three, but as its real loan rate was close to 0%, significantly below the normal level, the rising was just a returning to normal.

According to the study above, we can conclude that (1) the global real interest rates have strong consistency; (2) whether interest rate liberalization leads to rising interest rate depends on the global interest rate cycle and the domestic deviation from global rates; (3) the example of South Korea indicates that, besides the global rates cycle, the rising interest rate after liberalization also depends on the significantly depressed real rate before liberalization.

To sum up, if the real interest rate is depressed significantly and close to zero before liberalization, it inevitably surges sharply after full liberalization. Besides, due to the convergence of global interest rates, the domestic interest rate will be in line with global rates after liberalization.

How will interest rate change in China after interest rate liberalization?

In China, whether interest rate liberalization will lead to rising interest rate depends on (1) whether the real lending rate in China is significantly depressed and (2) the global interest rate cycle China is in. For the first factor, the real lending rate in China given by the World Bank is 4.2% in 2013, averaged 4.1% between 2012 and 2013, higher than the global average real lending rates. Based on the experience of India, Thailand, and Malaysia, if interest rate liberalization occurs in the flat stage of global interest rates and the domestic real lending rate is higher than the global rates pivot, the interest rate will not have the tendency to change after liberalization. For the second factor, the global real lending rates pivot is near 3%, in a relatively low point. If this lasts, it will create a favorable external environment for interest rate liberalization in China and the liberalization will not lead to rising interest rate.

One thing to note is that, China's real lending rate started to be higher than the global average in 2012. There was no significant difference between China's nominal lending rates during 2010–2011 and that in 2012. But due to the high inflation before 2012, the real rates were relatively low. As mentioned above, I think the inflation in China has entered into the fluctuation interval of 2–3%. Considering the nominal lending rate of 7%, the real lending rate will stay in the range of 4–5%, which indicates unobvious financial repression. The low inflation state in New Normal may be the reason why the central bank accelerates interest rate liberalization after 2013.

I suggested in "Asymmetric Interest Rate Liberalization effects," April 2014, that controls on loan interest rate have been lifted in 2013, the deposit rate, though still is controlled, has realized liberalization by financial products and money market funds. Statistically, interest rates moved upward in 2013 but declined sharply in 2014, indicating that interest rates have peaked. Assuming the economic growth and inflation to remain the same, the deposit rate should be located between the market-oriented deposit-like interest rate and the controlled one; the comprehensive interest rate will not change too much. Jin Zhongxia (the head of Research Bureau of PBOC) also proposed similar viewpoints in July 2014 in his article "The Bond Yield Curve and the Monetary Policy Transmission."

At last, we will discuss about four questions. (1) Why is financial repression not serious in China? (2) How can we understand the relationship between interest rate liberalization and the effort to lower financing cost by the State Council? (3) Why is there a relatively large spread between China's GDP and real lending rates? (4) How will the deposit rate change in the process of interest rate liberalization?

Why is financial depression in China less serious than market expectation? Reviewing the cycle chart of global interest rate, we can obviously discover that the real loan rate in the 1990s was often negative in China, which represents serious financial depression, and this situation also happened during 2003–2010. By observing the relationship between loan rate and CPI in China, we find that the reason lies in inflation (or the overheated economy at back). In the long run, the loan rate is highly stable.

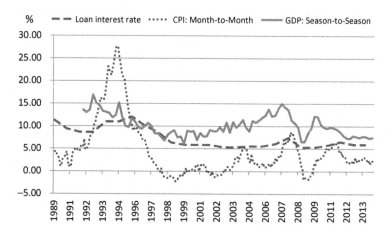

Figure 3.6 Loan interest rate in China is much more stable than GDP and CPI.

The pivot was 9–10% in the 1990s and 6% after 2000. The real loan rate was mainly determined by inflation. The inflation in China was typically caused by overheated economy. In the Old Normal, growth and inflation fluctuated frequently. Thus, with stable nominal loan rate, the real loan rate also fluctuated sharply. In the period of high inflation, the real rate was negative. In fact, the loan rate limited by government and divorced from the changing fundamentals was the performance of financial depression. After 2012, especially as the economy entered into the New Normal, inflation rate systematically fell back, and the real loan rate was compelled to rise, which led the real rate close to the market rate and eliminated the financial depression. As mentioned above, I suppose that considering that the real loan rate was not depressed much, interest rate liberalization will not lead to the rise of real rate and the nominal rate will fluctuate with the change of inflation.

How can we understand the relationship between interest rate liberalization and the effort of lowering the financing cost by the State Council? The most impressive event in market was the acceleration of the interest rate liberalization in 2013. In 2014, it turned to the effort of lowering the financing cost by the State Council. According to the mainstream opinion, these two targets are conflicting, for the acceleration of interest rate liberalization will lead to rising interest rate, while lowering financing cost is the administrative measure to lower interest rate. In my opinion, they are not contradictory in the New Normal. As mentioned above, I do not think that interest rate liberalization will push the interest rate upward. From the global aspect, as capital account is accelerating to liberalize, the higher real interest rate than other nations will attract inflow of global capital to lower the interest rate in China. From the domestic aspect, the real interest rate is too high for small and micro enterprises to bear, which is the direct reason of the effort of lowering the financing cost by the State Council. To some degree, this dilemma was caused by the structure of capital distribution in China. This topic, whether interest rate liberalization is simply lifting controls on deposit and lending rate, will be discussed in the next chapter. In that chapter, I will suggest that apart from the elimination of financial depression by interest rate liberalization, there is another reason that leads to the rising interest rate, the market failure and increasing systematic risk caused by the rising risk preference of financial institutions.

Why is there a relatively large spread between real loan rate and GDP in China? I think the reasons lie in these aspects. First, the non-standard high-yield assets are not included in the statistics of loan rate in China, so the real loan rate is underestimated. Second, banks' credit loan risk preference in China is lower than other nations and its non-performing loan ratios are lower than the average levels around the world. Third, we cannot exclude the slight depression in deposit rate which may be about 0–1% as I suppose. The spread will gradually diminish as GDP falls back.

How will the deposit rate change in the process of interest rate liberalization? As mentioned above, there is no certain relationship between interest rate liberalization and the fluctuation of interest rate. The movement of interest rate mainly depends on the current financial depression, the trend of long-term international interest rate and the specific domestic condition in the short term. In November 2014, interest rate cut was accompanied by enlarging the fluctuation interval, in which the deposit rate was reduced by 25 bps, while the floating capping was enlarged by 1.2 times and the upper limit maintained at 3.3%. This interest rate cut was different from previous ones. It did not intervene in the deposit and lending rate by administrative measures, but guided the market expectations in a relatively market-driven way. According to this policy, commercial banks could choose to operate at the upper limit of 3.3%, thus not affected by this policy. This interest cut was not compulsory in the deposit aspects. It mainly depended on the banks' independent choice. As to the consequence, the reaction among commercial banks was not accordant. Some stock-holding banks and city commercial banks adopted the way of floating to upper limit, so their deposit rate was even higher than previous. However, state-owned banks and other stock-holding banks lowered their deposit rate slightly. This phenomenon could be linked to the credit rationing in 2014. In 2014, traditional industries were in bad business condition and the non-performing loan ratio was climbing fast. To those large banks who examined strictly, there is shortage of superior assets and excess of deposit. What is more, their deposit deviations were even negative (Previously, absorbing deposit at the end of a month was common among banks. However, in late 2014, banks were releasing their deposits). The effects of enlarging the deposit rate fluctuation range prove that, there was no serious financial depression in China. On the contrary, deposit rate was too high before November 2014 and could not easily be lowered due to the Prisoner's Dilemma (Lack of homogeneous expectations, the bank cut down the interest rate first would face deposit outflow). It can be expected that the conditions would change when China's economy revives entirely, especially when the real estate industry recovers. And I suppose, deposit rate and bank financial products yield will converge in the future, with the former going up and the latter falling down. There will be no great change in banks' comprehensive cost, which mainly depends on current macroeconomic condition.

Chapter Four

New Objectives of Monetary Policy

The previous three chapters have discussed the differences between the "Old and New normal," restructuring the relationship between the government and the market and the approach to liberalize interest rates. The next three chapters will focus on the transformation of monetary policy framework by the central bank under the "New Normal." This framework consists of objectives, instruments and the transmission mechanism, which will be elaborated in the following three chapters.

This chapter focuses on the objectives of monetary policy. Generally speaking, these objectives consist of goals, intermediate targets and operating targets. The goals are what the central bank wants to achieve in the economy when making monetary policies, or the ultimate objective and reflection of policies. Intermediate targets are variables through which the central bank can observe and direct policy goals. Operating targets, or short-term indicators, are variables that the central bank can adjust through implementing instruments of monetary policy. To simplify the discussion, intermediate and operating targets are termed as "targets" and discussed as a whole in this book.

When the central bank makes monetary policy, it should identify the goals at first, then the instruments to achieve these goals. Instruments, however, cannot directly influence the goals. As a result, central bank introduces one or more variables (or "targets") that can be affected by the instruments to achieve the ultimate goals. The process looks like this:

$$\text{Instruments} \rightarrow \text{Targets} \rightarrow \text{Goals.}$$

In the discussion of central bank independence in Section One, my argument is that the Chinese central bank should be independent from financial authorities instead of the government. Section Two is about China's monetary policy goals. After a review of the "four goals" under the Old Normal, I suggest that the goal of equilibrium of the balance of payment be replaced with financial security, and discuss the central bank's choices under Mundell's Impossible Trinity. Section Three explores the reasons behind the shift from quantity-based to price-based targets, followed by the disadvantages of price-based targeting. At the end of this section is the possible approach to such shift. Section Four analyzes the rationality of excess reserve ratio as the market's indicator of capital abundance. In my opinion, the ration cannot reflect liquidity on the market, hence should not be taken by the central bank as a target.

SECTION ONE: SHOULD THE CENTRAL BANK BE INDEPENDENT?

It is generally agreed in western countries that the central bank should be highly independent. The underlying cause lies in the conflict between short-term goals of the government and long-term goals of the central bank. The government, motivated by short-term interests, i.e., to win more votes in the election, tends to expand fiscal expenditure and print more money to achieve temporary economic growth and low unemployment. This will result in inflation pressure in the long run, which is inconsistent with the primary goal of the central bank to maintain inflation at a reasonable level. Besides, an independent central bank is considered as a more credible policy-maker, which can achieve its goals more efficiently through desirable management.

But I do not see the necessity for the Chinese central bank to maintain independence given China's political regime. In fact, such independence is only necessary when the government and the central bank have conflicting goals. In other words, if the government pursues long-term goals, whether the central bank is independent is not that important. A major difference of China from western countries is its one-party system that ensures the Communist Party of China against other party competitors. The Chinese government, as a result, is less likely to be driven by short-term interests than its western counterparts. As a matter of fact, China's local governments are more like western countries' central government in their intention to adopt expansionary monetary policies, while the Chinese government is more like the central bank in the west.

The lesson of "4 trillion yuan stimulus" cannot justify independence of the central bank. A saying goes like this: the Chinese central bank was an "accomplice" in the government's over-stimulus; if the central bank was independent, "4 trillion yuan stimulus" and the resultant overcapacity would have been avoided. I do not agree with such a saying, since the launch of the stimulus package was a choice made at special times, not made in the government's own interests. In contrast, the FED, as a paragon of central bank independence, took similar measures, i.e., the QE, or commonly understood as "injecting liquidity," after the financial crisis broke out. In fact, the FED expanded its balance sheet by 300% from 2007 to 2013, while the Chinese central bank expanded only by 90% during the same period. From this, we can see that an independent central bank may also take extreme measures at special times.

We should not blindly believe that an independent bank is a good bank. Another example of the FED: its independence, instead of helping the US to avoid financial crisis in 2008, was held as the culprit of the crisis to some extent. As far as I am concerned, it is more likely to have a good central bank than have a good government in the west because western governments tend to maximize their short-term interests. In such case, the central bank should be independent from the government. But as the Chinese government pursues long-term interests, a good government is as likely as a good central bank. As a result, the central bank does not necessarily make better decisions than the government.

Whether the central bank should be independent from the government boils down to whether they have a shared goal. For the same goal, the government is more likely to make it happen because it has more resource and power than the central bank. In fact, the Chinese central bank is not independent in the traditional sense, because Law of the People's Republic of China on the People's Bank of China provides that the People's Bank of China is led by the State Council.

I believe, however, that the Chinese central bank should be independent from financial authorities. In the Old Normal, the economic cycle was directed not by the market, but by the government. Financial policy played a more important role than monetary policy, which meant the central bank was subordinate to financial authorities in the government's macroeconomic control. In the Old Normal, the government's macroeconomic control was mainly through stimulus, especially investment in infrastructure. During this process, the National Development and Reform Commission (NDRC) was responsible for examining and approving programs, while the central bank was responsible only for providing low-interest loans for these programs. The main approach for the central bank to influence the economy is to adjust the credit quota.

This model dated back to the period of planned economy: in the 1980s and earlier, the National Planning Commission (NPC) made the overall goal and task for the national economy; the Ministry of Finance (MOF) specified the use of money; and the People's Bank allocated the money. In such model, the central bank was responsible only for implementing decisions of the NPC and the MOF. For the central bank, there was no independence at all. As the central bank evolved, it began to be able to implement monetary policy by itself. However, the central bank is not fully independent in allocating credit quota, because credit quota is an important link between the NDRC, the MOF and the central bank.

According to the central bank's open information, it cancelled credit ceiling for state-owned commercial banks after 1998. In fact, the control is still in place. According to the vice president of Huaxia Bank, Huang Jinlao's *Necessity and Optimal Measures of Credit Control*, "in 2004 and 2005, new actual loans of commercial banks were less than the reference amount set by the central bank, but in 2006, 27% higher, and in 2007, 20% higher. In the fourth quarter of 2007, the central bank 'morally persuaded' major commercial banks to restrain loans. In 2008, the central bank brought back the credit ceiling and enforced the control for 10 months. In November 2008, to respond to the global financial crisis, the central bank lifted credit control. But only eight months later, in

July 2009, credit ceiling was resumed in practice." The central bank's guidance in loans is not appropriate for a market of liberalized interest rates. But as part of the central bank's monetary policy, such guidance is necessary in today's China where there are excessive capital demand, "soft" requirement on loans and misbehaviors of commercial banks. When stimulus is launched, however, since the amount of stimulus is determined by the State Council, the central bank's control on credit needs to be subordinate to the overall plan of ensuring a high GDP instead of its independent monetary policy.

In addition to credit scale, PBOC enjoys much independence in that it is technically responsible for stabilizing the value of RMB. Domestically, to stabilize RMB value means to control inflation while externally it means to maintain balance of international payments. Judging from the relation between the two rates — the reserve rate and benchmark lending and deposit rates — and inflation and growth, what the central bank targets at is inflation rather than growth. For instance, GDP growth kept dropping in 2011 but the bank continued to raise interest rate to curb the rising inflation. The rise of the required reserve rate was aimed at funds outstanding for foreign currency and inflation. Likewise in 2011, despite a drop in GDP growth, the bank increased the reserve rate multiple times to fight inflation and the influx of hot money. There is, of course, another explanation for this phenomenon: in 2011, China still enjoyed a growth rate near 10%, higher than the 8% government goal; there was no need to target growth back then. Under this explanation, the conclusion that the bank was targeting inflation still holds water. Externally, the bank balanced international payments by purchasing foreign reserves. In this way, RMB appreciated in an orderly manner and an export disaster caused by excess RMB appreciation was avoided.

The independency of monetary policy from fiscal policy can also be studied from the perspective of interest rate marketization. The bigger the role the market plays, the more independent the central bank will be from fiscal policy. International experience shows that when Keynesian economics prevailed, expansionary economic policy was adopted to boost demand and growth, giving more weight to the financial authorities. However, in the 1980s, when free market economics was the mainstream theory, central banks became more prominent as those in the Europe and

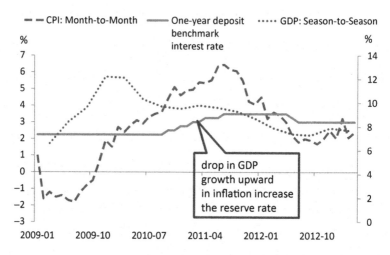

Figure 4.1   In 2011, when growth slowed down and inflation rose, PBOC raised interest rate, indicating its priority over the stability of RMB value. (Citation: WIND)

the US had much bigger impact on the economy than financial authorities. The role of China's central bank in macroeconomic control has also undergone changes. In the 1990s, when market reform was one of the government's priorities, the relation between the government and the market changed for the first time. In 1993, the State Council released *the Decision of the State Council on the Reform of the Financial System*, stating that one of the goals of the financial structure reform is "to set up a macroeconomic-regulatory system of the central bank that implements independently the monetary policy under the leadership of the State Council." In the same year, Zhu Rongji, the then Vice Premier of the State Council, took the office of governor of the People's Bank of China, giving the bank more independency. Hu–Wen Administration emphasized the role of the government, giving less play to the market. The NDRC was put at the helm of macroeconomic control with clear marks of planned economy while PBOC's monetary policy was only a supplement with dwindling independency. In 2013, *Decision of the CCCPC on Some Major Issues Concerning Comprehensively Deepening the Reform* of the third Plenary Session of the 18th CPC Central Committee declares "the market should play a decisive role in allocating resources." One of the primary conditions for this is less intervention from the government. Since then, taking steps to streamline administration and delegate power has been a key measure of the new administration to boost economy. Accordingly, the central bank has enjoyed more prominence in the top design of the nation. The liberalization of interest rate and exchange rate accelerates; new monetary tools keep emerging; monetary policy has even been introduced into the reform of industrial structure, a former territory of fiscal policy. It should also be noted that Zhou was elected Vice Chairman of CPPCC, a sub-national leader just as Zhu in the late 1990s. In both times, the relation between the government and the market was reshaped and the status of the bank increased. As interest rate liberalization proceeds, monetary policy will be more independent from fiscal policy.

SECTION TWO: REFORM ON GOALS — THE NEW FOUR-GOAL REGIME

In this section, I will introduce the goals in the Old Normal, namely the Four-Goal Regime and then elaborate on the reasons why financial security should be one of the goals of monetary policies. Then I will propose the standpoint that as exchange rate enters the range of balance, the equilibrium in the balance of payments should no longer be set as one goal of monetary policies. Finally, this section will discuss the options of China's central bank in Mundell's Impossible Trinity.

Goals in the Old Normal

The transition of the goals of China's monetary policies

There has been a big controversy over the goals of China's central bank, including: first, should there be one single goal or multiple goals? Second, what goals should be chosen?

The representative of "single goal" is the Inflation Targeting Regime, which has been very popular among central banks since the 1990s, adopted by the United Kingdom, New Zealand, Canada, Australia, Mexico, Sweden and other countries. Its main characteristic is that the monetary authority releases to the public explicitly its inflation targets for a relatively long time and takes proactive measures to maintain the price level

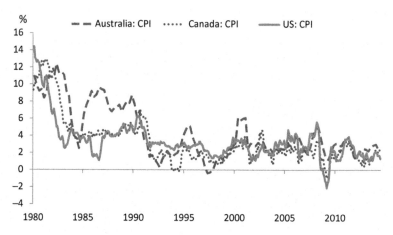

Figure 4.2   The United States is not an Inflation Targeting Regime, but its inflation level is not high compared to inflation targeting countries. (Citation: WIND)

close to the targets. The measurable are usually Consumer Price Index (CPI) and core CPI. Its main advantage is that market entities have steady expectations for future market and the expectations will lower inflation so that the cost of inflation management can be reduced. Adopting the Inflation Targeting Regime can reduce inflation volatility, control inflation and maintain steady growth in these countries.

However, some economists do not believe this is the right option, mainly for two reasons: (1) the global low inflation since the 1990s is attributed to less volatility in oil price, technological advancement and more supply of primary products by developing countries; it is probably not the effect of the Inflation Targeting Regime; (2) the financial crisis in 2008 indicates that focusing on inflation (or economic growth) alone does not guarantee steady growth and that more complicated goals and regulation instruments are required.

China's central bank has also gone through the controversy over single goal and multiple goals, especially before the release of *Decision on the Reform of Financial System* (*Decision*) in 1993 and *Law of the People's Republic of China on the People's Bank of China* (*Law on the People's Bank of China*) in 1995. The Decision provides that "the goals of monetary policies are to maintain currency stability and thereby promote economic growth." In the Law on the People's Bank of China in 1995, the provision was revised as follows: "the goals of monetary policies are to maintain the stability of currency value and thereby promote economic growth." The provision was kept the same in the revised version of the Law on the People's Bank of China in 2003. Although "promote economic growth" is not the primary, direct goal of monetary policies, it is still regarded as one of the goals as stated in the provision. Since then, although there is still no consensus over whether China should have multiple goals, it has become an agreed fact that China's central bank is a multiple-goal regime.

Since then, the academic controversy over the goals of monetary policies have been focused on two issues: first, the definition of "the stability of currency value"; and second, whether China has two goals or multiple goals.

The connotations of "the stability of currency value" are in constant extension. In early years, the stability of currency value was equal to curtailing inflation, but later it also brought in deflation control and stable exchange rate of RMB, etc. In 2007, Yi Gang, the then Assistant Governor and incumbent Deputy Governor of the People's Bank of China, gave an authoritative and widely recognized explanation for the stability of currency value — "the stability of RMB value has two implications: first, inflation control so as to stabilize domestic purchasing power; and second, maintain the stability of RMB's exchange rate at a reasonable and balanced level to ensure external stability."

There has been a lot of discussion on the choice of two goals and multiple goals. In 2000, Xie Ping, the then Director of the Research Bureau of the People's Bank of China, suggested that the goals of China's monetary policies include "stabilizing price, promoting employment, ensuring economic growth, supporting the reform of state-owned enterprises, increasing domestic demand in accordance with proactive fiscal policies, preventing the decrease of foreign exchange reserve and maintaining the stability of RMB exchange rate." Zhou Xiaochuan has reiterated in many occasions that China's central bank is a four-goal regime — maintaining inflation at a low level, promoting economic growth, ensuring high employment rate and guaranteeing the equilibrium of the balance of international payments" ("The Goals and the Instrument Options of Monetary Policies," Zhou Xiaochuan, 2011). Although there is no clear legal provision that China has changed from "two goals" to "four goals," the attitude of central bank officials and the practice of monetary policies have clearly indicated the transition.

In "The Goals of Monetary Policies and Crisis Responsive Measures" and "The Goals and the Instrument Options of Monetary Policies," Zhou Xiaochuan explained that the reasons for adopting a four-goal regime was "the special circumstances during China's economic reform and transformation" and "the less effective Inflation Targeting Regime in current situation." The first reason means: first, too much emphasis on low inflation targets of the People's Bank of China may hinder government's price reform; second, Inflation Targeting Regime is mainly based on hypotheses like Efficient Market Hypothesis, which dos not fully suit China. In addition, economic growth, low inflation and employment may not be compatible at some time. A single Inflation Targeting Regime cannot meet the demands of all stakeholders; and third, structural change during economic transformation is a typical phenomenon and the structural reform is yet to be deepened. They will hinder the optimization of monetary policy targeting function. Therefore, the Inflation Targeting Regime does not suit China. In addition, the academia started to question the regime *per se* after the financial crisis and this is also an important reason for China to deny Inflation Targeting Regime.

I take the view that adopting a four-goal regime is fundamentally attributed to China's political system. In 2002, the Report of the 16th CPC Congress clarifies for the first time that "the goals of macro control are promoting economic growth, increasing employment, stabilizing price and maintaining the equilibrium of the balance of international payments." The four goals are in line with the mainstream view of modern western economics on macroeconomic policies (*Western Economics*, Gao Hongye, 2000). In the last section, I proposed that China's central bank and Chinese government have similar goals for monetary policies due to the uniqueness of China's political system. It is less necessary to maintain China's currency independent of that of western countries. Therefore, it is appropriate for China's central bank to adopt the same four goals as the macroeconomic control of the Chinese government.

A general introduction of the Four-Goal regime

(a) Stabilizing commodity prices

Generally speaking, stabilizing commodity prices is the primary goal of central bank's monetary policies. If a country sees major fluctuation in commodity price, the functions of monetary policies and the performance of national economy will be jeopardized. Controlling inflation is a major measure for stabilizing prices. Therefore, inflation rate has become an index measuring the stability of prices. According to international experience, three major indexes are used to measure inflation level: first, GDP deflator, which measures the ultimate products and services in GDP and reflects the changes in their prices; second, CPI, which measures consumers' daily expenses and reflects the changes in consumer prices; and third, Wholesale Price Index (WPI), which measures wholesale trades and reflects the changes in the price of commodities.

(b) Full employment

In Keynesian economics, full employment refers to a state in which, except for normal temporary unemployment (structural unemployment caused by job changes and frictional unemployment caused by information asymmetry), the whole population in economic activity has access to suitable jobs without labor force waste. When the human resource achieves full employment, non-human resources are also fully utilized and the real output of the whole national economy approaches or even equals potential output. In this situation, unemployment level is named Natural Rate of Unemployment or "Non-accelerating Inflation Rate of Unemployment." According to Keynesian economics, real unemployment rate fluctuates around the axis of the Natural Rate of Unemployment, and the fluctuation forms economic cycles.

In application, most countries use the unemployment rate obtained through sampling survey of labor force (Survey Unemployment Rate) to measure the employment level of labor force. The unemployment rate shows how far the society is from full employment. Bigger difference between real unemployment rate and natural unemployment rate means weaker economic growth. Therefore, all countries are lowering unemployment to a rational level to achieve the goals of economic growth. In most cases, the reason behind non-full employment is the cyclical unemployment caused by weak demand. As the aggregate supply exceeds the aggregate demand, the economic resources (including labor force resource) in a society cannot be properly and fully utilized. During economic crisis and recession, cyclical unemployment is an especially significant phenomenon. According to western economics, except for weak demand, other reasons for unemployment such as structural unemployment caused by job changes and frictional unemployment caused by information asymmetry are inevitable.

A big problem for China now is the absence of a reliable employment index. The USA uses unemployment rate or non-Agricultural Employment Index to measure employment and the data is widely recognized by economists and the market. China, however, only has a monthly index named Urban Newly Employed Population. This index was adopted in 2013. It exhibits significant seasonality and cannot be used for any valuable analysis. Seasonal indexes including Urban Registered Unemployment and Urban Unemployed Population are widely criticized. For example, from 2011 September to 2013 June, Urban Registered Unemployment rate remained at 4.1% and this is unrealistic. As employment becomes increasingly important in China's monetary policy and macro control, a reliable employment index is badly needed.

(c) Economic growth

Economic growth determines long-term development trends of production and living standard. In general, the index that countries use to measure economic growth is the annual increase rate of real gross national product, namely, the increased rate of GNP adjusted for inflation. In the long run, GNP must rise at a reasonable speed instead of exceeding the growth potential of economy. While in the short term, if idle capacity exists, to expand money supply can stimulate total demand, and thus create more jobs and boost output. As expansionary monetary policy promotes short-term economic growth, it is considered as an effective measure. However, if there is little growth potential, when money supply increases, "money illusion" may cause labor wage to grow slower than money supply, which means a decrease in labor cost. In this way, investment and economic growth will be promoted in the short term, but in the long run, inflation will rise.

Therefore, a central bank's goal of achieving economic growth means that when fixed objectives are met, the central bank uses its tools to optimize resource distribution and promote economic growth. Generally, the central bank can boost investment through expanding money supply or cutting down real interest rate; or eliminate uncertainties caused by investments through curbing inflation rate, and change investment in real economy through managing inflation expectation.

(d) Equilibrium of Balance of Payments (BOP)

First of all, I would like to introduce the balance of payments (BOP). BOP reflects all of a country's economic transactions with the rest of the world for a specific period, involving trade contacts, non-trade contacts, cash transfer and changes in reserve assets. According to accounting rules, BOP is composed of four sub-accounts: current account, capital account, reserve account and error and omissions. Under every sub-account, all transactions are divided into autonomous transaction and accommodating transaction: an autonomous transaction refers to an economic transaction that happens autonomously due to economic purpose, political consideration or moral motivation, such as trade, aid, donation and foreign exchange; an accommodating transaction refers to a transaction that is undertaken to cover deficit or surplus in autonomous transactions, such as acquiring short-term financing from international financial institutions, or using domestic gold reserve or foreign exchange reserve to correct the disequilibrium.

Balance of payments generally refers to the balance in autonomous transactions of a country. If in autonomous transactions, income exceeds expenses, we call it surplus; otherwise, we call it deficit. Both surplus and deficit in the long run, will lead to imbalance of BOP.

To balance international payments means to correct imbalance of BOP through various measures. The imbalance, no matter surplus or deficit, will impact domestic economy. Huge long-term deficit will cause foreign exchange reserve to plummet and result in heavy debts and great interest burden while huge long-term surplus will lead to resource waste and idle foreign currency, and particularly, if the central bank issues more money in response to increasing foreign currency, it will cause or exacerbate inflation. Of course, compared to surplus, deficit has worse impacts, thus all countries make more efforts to reduce and even eliminate deficit to adjust BOP.

Inner links among the "four goals"

Although many central banks would like to achieve multiple goals, realizing economic growth, full employment and equilibrium of BOP on the basis of price stability, relationships between these four goals are complex. Theoretically, the four goals are not consistent with each other, thus to take the best monetary policy, central banks must find a balance.

(a) Full employment and economic growth

Okun's law describes stable relationships between GDP growth rate and unemployment rate: the difference between unemployment rate and its natural rate has a negative relationship with the difference between real GDP and potential GDP, indicating that the closer the real growth rate is to the potential rate, the closer will be the unemployment rate to the natural rate. However, economic growth follows various models. Except for the labor-intensive model, other models (resource-intensive, capital-intensive, knowledge-intensive), to some extent, contradict full employment.

In China, growth is mainly driven by investment; thus Okun's law does not fit the country's situation well. What is more important, structural factors are important elements that affect China's unemployment rate. The same quantity of GDP can be produced by different amounts of people. Generally, the service industry needs a larger labor force. This is why the year 2014 witnessed a slower growth rate but more new jobs in urban areas than the previous year.

(b) Price stability and economic growth

In theory, inflation and economic growth can supplement each other: only when the money market is stable can the financial environment be sound and the economy develop in a sustainable, stable and coordinated way;

only when the economy grows can the total social demand and supply be balanced and monetary stability guaranteed. But China's experience shows that, given its capital shortage, big demand for investment, and great employment pressure, monetary stability has always been sacrificed. Rapid economic growth is supported by excessive money supply, which will lead to rising inflation, excess capacity and inventory backlog; high inflation rate will in turn force the central bank to tighten monetary policy and thus slow down economic growth.

The relationship between economic growth and inflation is positive, the realization of "low inflation, high growth" must be based on potential growth. Economic development that exceeds potential growth will definitely cause increasing inflation rate. In order to curb inflation, we must first control excessive economic growth.

(c) Price stability and full employment

In order to study the relationship between unemployment rate and inflation rate, we must use an important macroeconomic variable — natural rate of unemployment. Natural rate of unemployment is a "benchmark" to evaluate unemployment rate in an economy, the difference between actual rate and natural rate is an effective index to measure inflation pressure in economy.

William Phillips *et al.,* pioneers in the study over the relationship between inflation and unemployment rate, found an inverse relationship between inflation and unemployment rate — the "Phillips Curve." Later studies show that if the government tries to maintain low unemployment rate through higher inflation rate, the inverse relationship would disappear. In other words, unemployment rate in the long term cannot be lower than a specific level — the natural rate of unemployment, a rate of unemployment when the labor market is in equilibrium under current economic structure. The natural rate of unemployment and the potential GDP have the same break-even point. This indicates that if a country wants to control inflation and reduce inflation rate, it must bear a relatively high unemployment rate, that is, it must sacrifice one goal when taking monetary policies. Currently, the ultimate goal of the US Federal Reserve's monetary policy is "full employment and price stability." The FED's choice of a final monetary policy is the trade-off between unemployment and inflation.

(d) Price stability and balance of payments

Price stability always clashes with balance of payments. Price stability is an internal target of monetary policy, and balance of payments is an external target. Given the inconsistency of the two targets and the influence of terms of trade, it is hard for a country to meet both internal and external targets at the same time.

Sometimes, in order to balance international payments, external devaluation measures may be taken which exacerbate domestic inflation. Sometimes, in order to rescue public finance from the brink of failure, more money may be issued, which also causes inflation. In the case of inflation, in order to stabilize prices and increase domestic supply, import must be increased and export cut down, which will lead to payment deficit. And then in order to correct this disequilibrium and narrow the deficit, policies must be taken to expand export and reduce import. These policies will increase foreign currency reserve, expand money base and money supply, and will in turn increase inflation pressure, rise prices and thus impact price stability.

(e) Economic growth and balance of payments

Economic growth and balance of payments are both consistent and contradictory. First, normally, economic growth helps increase the competitiveness of domestic products in the global market, making the nation a better exporter. Second, promoting economic growth can always increase national income, people's demand for products and people's purchasing power. As import is an increasing function of domestic revenue and national income, economic growth will lead import to rise. Third, in order to promote economic growth, investment must be increased by motivating domestic savings and also by attracting foreign capital through all measures. This differs from former measures in that, strengthening the usage of foreign capital may cause deficit in capital account and bring difficulties in balancing economic growth with balance of payments. In order to balance the deficit, measures are taken to cut down aggregate domestic demand, and rely less on import, but these measures will in turn affect domestic economic growth.

"Financial Security" Should be a Goal

In my opinion, in the "New Normal" economy, "financial security" should be a goal of the central bank's monetary policy. Relevant topics have been discussed for a long time. For example, before 2008, people widely discussed whether "price of financial assets" should be a goal of the central bank's monetary policy, i.e., whether central banks should pay attention to asset price bubbles. Central banks and the academic mainstream believed that financial asset price should not be a goal. In "Foreigner Central Bankers' Opinion on Monetary Policy and Asset Price," a special column of "Monetary Policy Implementation Report" for the second quarter in 2007, the Central Bank of China pointed out that central bankers like Bernanke of the FED, and Trichet of the ECB all think that "asset price should not become a goal of monetary policy." But after the 2008 financial crisis, central bankers all over the world began to rethink and put forward a macroprudential framework to supplement monetary policy. At the same time, central banks have taken "financial stability" as a working priority, and "stability" is not restricted to the "stability of financial asset price."

I think the concept "financial stability" is still worth discussing. This concept is against "financial fragility," but "stability" itself has more meanings. Literally, "financial stability" means to control financial volatility, but this is obviously not the central bank's duty. Problems concerning economic growth, inflation and employment can be solved through counter-cyclical operation — using moderately loose monetary policy to curb big fluctuations in macro-economy. It is reasonable to put forward "stability," but for finance, fluctuations are normal. It is meaningless to control financial volatility. In fact, what needs to be prevented in the financial system is just "financial risks," a concept opposite to "financial security." Thus, I think "financial security" is more appropriate.

Now allow me to explain why I believe that "financial security" should be a goal of monetary policy. Then, I will discuss asset price bubble and whether it is reasonable to adjust asset prices through interest rate policy.

Financial security should be one of the goals

Financial security used to be inferred in fundamentals, but it has become an independent variable along with interest rate liberalization. In the Old Normal, risk preference and asset-price bubbles, as dependent variables, fluctuated with the economic cycle. Financial risks were more likely caused by economic breakdown. In the New Normal, mixed operation becomes the trend. With accelerated interest rate liberalization, financial innovations are more complex. Financial risks are no longer inferred in fundamentals, best exemplified in the US financial crisis. As the lender of last resort, the central bank should intervene in advance. Seen from international experience, after the financial crisis bursts, central banks need to implement rescue measures to avoid further damage to the entire economy. This will lead to issues like "too big to fall." With the responsibility to rescue, the central bank should also be entitled to regulate the rescued beforehand, or there will be moral hazard in financial institutions.

• Macro fundamentals fluctuate much less than before. Bounded within the upper and lower limits set by the government, growth and inflation fluctuate in a narrow range and account for less operations of the central bank's monetary policy. From 2000 to 2012, the GDP swung widely between 6% and 15%, sometimes even so in a single year. For example, the quarterly GDP for 2010 were 12.1%, 10.3%, 9.7%, and 9.5%. Although the fluctuation narrowed in 2011, the range was 1% within the year, and the GDP grew by 9.8%, 9.6%, 9.3%, and 8.7% quarterly. Since 2013, the GDP fluctuated only within 7.4% to 7.8%, narrowed greatly. From 2000 to 2012, CPI swung between –2% and 9%, with an obvious inflation cycle of every other two to four years. The highest growth rate of pork price was 80% year-on-year, proving a clearly "pork cycle." Since 2013, pork price fluctuated within ±10%, and CPI within 1.8% to 3.2%, also much narrower than before. This is due to the clear upper and lower bounds set by the government, and the industrialization and digitization. When growth and inflation fluctuate in a narrow range, it is more feasible for the central bank to focus on other goals of its monetary policy.

• Since 2013, with significantly boosted interest rate liberalization, coupled with financial reform as a priority for the government and the central bank, financial systemic risk gains more importance. On July 19, 2013,

PBOC announced that with the approval of the State Council, it would deregulate the loan interest rates for financial institutions from July 20, 2013. On December 8, 2013, PBOC published *Interim Measures for Interbank Deposit Management*. NCD (Negotiable certificate of Deposit) since then became an official tool for managing banking liquidity. Judging from the words of the management, deposit insurance system was very likely to be introduced in 2014. On July 10, 2014, Zhou Xiaochuan said that China would realize interest rate liberalization within two years. During such liberalization, competition within the financial system will grow significantly. For example, in the US, from 1960 to 1980, less than 10 banks closed annually; but during interest rate liberalization in the 1980s, the number of closed banks grew rapidly, more than 200 annually by the end of the 80s. This brought huge risks to the US financial system.

• With the emergence of high-yield riskless financial innovations like "the non-standard," market failure will lead to risk externalization. Since 2012, the rebound of real estate and the boom of infrastructure investment have driven up economy, a time ready for financial institutions to increase leverage. Meanwhile, "the non-standard" emerged in real estate, infrastructure, and over-capacity industries. As a result, a lot of capital flew into these earlier restricted areas. These industries are pro-cyclical: when economy is growing, their risk for default is low. Due to asset-price bubbles and soft intervention, these industries can afford financial costs much higher than ordinary companies, hence providing very high yields for banks. This gives birth to high-yield riskless assets for banks. "The non-standard" and alike services emerged in 2012, and grew rapidly in the first half of 2013. By the end of Q3 in 2012, in total social financing, both trust and entrusted loans were fewer than 180 billion yuan monthly, with an average of 140 billion yuan. The number surged since the end of 2012 with the monthly average over 360 billion yuan by the end of Q2 in 2013, and over 600 billion yuan in March. While "the non-standard" is expanding, growth and inflation fluctuate within a narrow range; if the central bank only targets growth and inflation, financial systemic risk will accumulate rapidly, eventually causing a financial crisis.

• As the lender of last resort, the central bank should intervene financial risks in advance. World experience shows that to match the role as the last lender, central banks should have regulatory power. In 2010, Obama signed Dodd-Frank Act. In a time of strengthening regulation, the act gave the Federal Reserve much more power to regulate, and identified the Fed's central role in national systemic risk management and financial regulation. Specifically, in terms of financial regulation, the Fed was explicitly given the macroprudential regulatory power to safeguard financial stability; the prudential regulatory power of the Fed over financial institutions was strengthened and extended; the responsibilities to protect consumers were consolidated from scattered financial regulatory institutions to the Bureau of Consumer Financial Protection located inside the Fed.

Measures against asset price bubbles

Scholars dispute whether the central bank should regulate by targeting property price or financial systemic risks, mainly in the following points:

- The central bank does not have more information or capacity than the market to identify systemic risks earlier.
- With interest rate policy, the central bank cannot multi-task: stabilizing the fluctuation of inflation and economy, and meanwhile price fluctuation in financial market. Controlling asset price might harm the innocent.
- Asset price may change greatly within a short term. For example, stock price might rise markedly in a month and fall markedly in the following month. Monetary policies based on short-term fluctuation are unreasonable.
- Tightened policy against asset bubbles might accelerate the burst of bubbles; raising interest rate might increase the risk of financial instability. Therefore, using interest rates to intervene asset price might lead to higher risks than yields.

Before the financial crisis in 2008, the above disputes prevented the central bank from targeting asset price or financial systemic risks. After the crisis, scholars presented convincing answers to these issues, hence putting systemic risks under the central bank's attention:

• In Frederic Mishkin's theory, asset price bubbles fall into two categories: the boom bubble, and the pure irrational exuberance bubble. I think the distinction lies in whether it is a collateral bubble, i.e., when collateral price increases, will the bubble create a pro-cyclical effect and drive up leverage. The credit boom bubble is a price rise driven by credit boom. The asset price rise encourages further lending against these assets, leading to a credit boom followed by a price rise. This creates a positive feedback loop, involving higher leverage and amplified risks. The subprime crisis in 2008 is an example. The pure irrational exuberance bubble is driven by over-optimistic expectations, similar to Keynes's animal spirits. This bubble is hard for central banks to identify, but since it is driven by speculative funds, its burst does much less damage, hence no need for intervention, like the US Internet bubble. For the boom bubble, the central bank can access credit banks' data for far more capacity to identify bubbles, therefore determining the presence and severity of bubbles ahead of the market.

• Indeed, the central bank cannot multi-task, but it does not prevent the central bank from having multiple goals. Actually, the four goals, i.e., growth, inflation, employment, and balance of international payments, are impossible to fulfill at the same time. However, the central bank can focus on primary contradictions, and set ranges to maintain these targets at relatively stable and reasonable levels.

• Taking financial systemic risks as one of the goals does not mean that the central bank should focus on asset-price bubbles or systemic risks like it did on growth and inflation, because reaction functions of interest rate policy vary on different targets. For short-term high volatility, the central bank should not intervene but observe. If it remains abnormal for a certain period of time, and if studies of its mechanism prove the presence of severe bubbles, the central bank should intervene.

• If intervention through monetary policy is at the cost of other institutions' interim interest, the damage should be compared with that of no intervention. The financial crisis in 2008 showed that the burst of financial systemic risks has profound and lasting damages to global economy, much severer than what tightening monetary policy would do to other institutions. Therefore, for a pure irrational exuberance bubble, its subtle damage requires no monetary policy; for a credit boom bubble, the central bank should implement timely measures against systemic risks.

Should interest rate policy target asset price?

After the financial crisis in 2008, introspection of central banks worldwide focuses on the fact that their regulatory power does not match their role as the lender of last resort. Before the crisis, central banks had no regulatory power, but after the crisis, they are responsible for bailouts. This is unreasonable. Macroprudential framework hence drew great attention and was widely researched. In theory, adopting macroprudential measures and strengthening regulation are the most effective and proper ways to solve financial systemic risks. However, things are more complicated in practice, and that is why we should employ interest rate policy to intervene asset-price bubbles.

• Money market interest rate involves financial systemic risks, so regulation on interest rate is reasonable. Like the money shortage in 2013, soaring interest rates reflected an increase of systemic risks. If the central bank employs price-based operation, and its monetary policy regards money market interest rate as an intermediate target, what choice should the central bank make? If the central bank is aware of the increased systemic risks, but still maintains the same money market interest rate (based on traditional Taylor rule, it should be so), excessive leverage by financial institutions may lead to a subprime crisis, like in the US. In this way, interest rate mechanism in money market involves systemic risks, and the central bank's target is exactly money market interest rate, so the central bank's operation should target systemic risks.

• Macroprudential regulation over financial systemic risks has serious time lag. The focus of such regulation lies in the coordination between the central bank and other institutions in solving systemic risks. However, coordination requires time, and participants may have disputes. Should the central bank just wait and do nothing? For example, the state council introduced regulatory policy by the end of 2013, but the central bank acquired regulatory power in May 2014, almost a year after the money shortage on June 20 last year. Before progress was made in macroprudential regulation, the central bank could only manage systemic risks through monetary policy, i.e., raising interest rates and amplifying volatility.

- Intervention through monetary policy is at the cost of other institutions' interim interest, but less damaging than the burst of financial systemic risks, as explained earlier. Specifically, the burst of credit boom bubbles is far more severe than the interim cost to other institutions. Before the macroprudential regulation takes effect, interest rate policy has more potential benefits than inaction.

However, the central bank should not constantly use interest rate tools to manage financial systemic risks or asset-price bubbles. Based on the revised Taylor rule, the reaction function to financial systemic risks is different from that to growth and inflation. The reaction to systemic risks is a threshold piecewise function: only when systemic risks accumulate to a certain threshold will interest rate policy be used for intervention. I divided financial systemic risk into three levels.

- **Level 1**: The risk remains low, and the central bank will not use monetary policy against it.

- **Level 2**: The risk grows due to liberalization. The central bank will observe and evaluate the risk, and determine the causes and whether the risk touches the bottom line to burst. If the cause is normal fluctuation of the market, the central bank will remain inactive.

- **Level 3**: The risk grows rapidly, and the cause is market failure or other factors that the market fails to self-correct. The central bank will first intervene by raising benchmark rate and amplifying market interest rate volatility, and then work with other institutions to promote macroprudential framework to treat the root cause.

"Balance of International Payments" Should not Remain a Goal

"Balance of international payments" has long been a goal of the central bank's monetary policy in China. Zhou Xiaochuan, governor of BPOC, emphasized its significance to the bank repeatedly in different occasions. However, in my opinion, its significance is declining. If we can successfully adopt a managed floating exchange rate regime, balance of international payments would no longer have to be one of the "four goals" of monetary policy.

As far as I am concerned, balance of international payments was made an independent goal due to substantial under-valuation of RMB and the double surplus situation. Specifically, the managed floating exchange rate regime China has adopted is more like a fixed exchange rate regime in practice, which I refer to as "an exchange rate regime similar to the fixed ones." Under such regime, RMB could appreciate unilaterally, preventing export companies from catastrophic consequences brought by over-speed RMB appreciation. The fourth part of this section will further elaborate the Impossible Trinity and balance of payments. The central bank's policy on exchange rate cannot be implemented through other policies, i.e., exchange rate changes are independent of economic growth, inflation, and employment; thus the central bank must continue to keep balance of international payments as an independent goal. Meanwhile, funds outstanding for foreign exchange, still the dominant form of injection, impact enormously on domestic money supply, inflation and export. Therefore, when RMB is substantially underestimated and its exchange rate is reaching equilibrium, it is necessary to take balance of international payments as one of the goals.

However, when RMB exchange rate has reached equilibrium, and the central bank has withdrawn more from the routine intervention of foreign exchanges leaving wider space for exchange rate fluctuation, the importance of "balance of international payments" is significantly declined. China's exchange rate policy is shifting to a floating one. According to international experience, balance of international payments can be reached under a floating exchange rate regime, for example, foreign exchange reserves of US and EU countries remain basically unchanged. Under a floating exchange rate regime, exchange rate is no longer an independent variable, but is dependent upon national fundamentals such as growth and inflation. But I do not believe that the central bank should never react to international capital flow. Non-routine intervention of foreign exchanges that other central banks usually adopt is aiming to fend off financial risks, rather than to achieve balance of international payments like China. Therefore, when we have economic growth, high employment, low inflation and financial security as the "four new goals" of monetary policy, balance of international payments will be reached in the process of achieving these four goals, and it is not necessary to be an independent goal.

Currently, more research concerning BOP focuses on which BOP structure is more favorable to China. Some argue that China should maintain a deficit in the capital account to avoid interest payment caused by foreign capital inflow. I disagree with this point. A deficit in the capital account will be beneficial only when foreign technologies and talents are introduced instead of hot money; similarly, when the capital outflow only takes form of investment in authorized economic operators or in mergers and acquisitions of technology companies, a surplus in the capital account will maximize domestic interest. These issues are relevant to national economic strategies including how to encourage foreign investment and how to use funds outstanding for foreign exchange rather than the BOPs. Therefore, it should no longer be a goal of monetary policy since it is less important compared with other goals.

Central Bank's Choices in the "Impossible Trinity"

The "Impossible Trinity" is a trilemma which states that it is impossible to have all three of the following objectives at the same time, namely, an independent monetary policy, a fixed exchange rate and free capital flow. As previously mentioned, China's monetary policy is more independent compared with foreign central banks; hence the central bank of China must forgo one of the latter two objectives. As far as I am concerned, in the Old Normal, the central bank of China kept monetary policy independent, adopted an exchange rate regime similar to fixed ones, and imposed relatively strict capital control.

First, what is an exchange rate regime similar to fixed ones? According to official statement, China adopts "a managed floating exchange rate regime" which I think is similar to a fixed exchange rate regime in practice. In the beginning of the exchange rate reform, substantial underestimation of RMB coupled with influx of hot money caused "double surplus," which means foreign currency flows into both current account and capital account. Fundamentally speaking, the reason is that balance of international payment must be achieved through enhanced

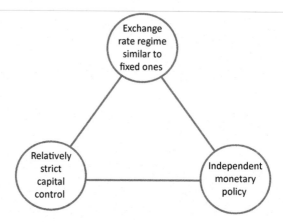

Figure 4.3   China's choices in the "Impossible Trinity" in the Old Normal.

market operations by the central bank under a fixed exchange rate regime. On the contrary, if double surplus happens in a floating exchange rate regime, it will lead to domestic currency appreciation, hence result in lower export, higher import, and bigger trade surplus; meanwhile, hot money influx to capital account will plunge when domestic currency is no longer underestimated. However, China adopts an exchange rate regime similar to the fixed ones rather than a floating one, i.e., the central bank admits the trend of RMB appreciation, but will control the speed of its appreciation by setting central parity rate and exchange rate fluctuation range, thus a fixed exchange rate regime with changing exchange rate targets has taken shape, which I refer to as an "exchange rate regime similar to fixed ones." The advantage of this regime is that, during the process of interest rate liberalization, it can prevent considerable appreciation of RMB in a short term, which will be a hard blow to export companies and financial market stability.

Now allow me to explain the term relatively strict capital control. In case of double surplus, why not impose full control on capital account to maintain a fixed exchange rate? I think there are three reasons for that. First, the price is too high; second, foreign capital is needed to provide China with advanced technologies and managerial experience; third, it cannot reverse the trend of RMB appreciation when the foreign reserves accumulated by huge trade surplus can no longer be spent through channels in the market. Therefore, the central bank imposes relatively stringent capital controls, curbing hot money inflows to some extent.

Under an exchange rate regime similar to fixed ones, the central bank must conduct foreign exchange settlement and sale at a certain target interest rate at any time point (even though the target is in constant change in the long run). The central bank buys up the foreign exchange flows into China in double surplus to balance BOP account. The purchased foreign exchanges form foreign exchange reserve. Then the central bank uses the foreign exchange reserve in international market like purchasing US government bonds, so that the foreign exchanges flow into China in double surplus equals that outflow through the central bank. This is why "balance of international payments" is one of the four goals of monetary policy in the Old Normal. Under a purely floating exchange rate system, the central bank does not intervene through foreign exchange transactions except that in case of financial crises or international hot money attacks, balance of BOP account is reached automatically through appreciation or devaluation of its currency.

When the central bank adopts an exchange rate regime similar to fixed ones, and imposes relatively strict capital control, monetary policy can be independent. First, I will explain why the central bank cannot adopt independent monetary policy while pursuing fixed exchange rate and free capital flow. If two countries have independent monetary policy and there is a gap between their interest rate, hot money will flow into the one with higher interest rate, and the hot money will convert into domestic currency at a fixed exchange rate, which means infinite quantity of base currency injection to the home country. As a result, its interest rate declines until the gap disappears. But under relatively strict capital control, the central bank could control the quantity of base currency injection to meet interest rate target, thus maintaining monetary policy independence. In other words, when capital flows freely, the central bank needs to withdraw infinite quantity of base currency, and the cost to do so is unbearably high (the central bank needs to issue infinite quantity of central bank bills, or to raise reserve ratio to near 100%); but within certain limits, it is possible to maintain monetary policy independence through withdrawal of excessive base currency. In practice, in times of huge foreign currency inflow, the central bank could control excessive base currency by raising reserve ratio or issuing central bank bills and maintaining monetary policy independence.

Finally, what is monetary policy independence? To maintain monetary policy independence is to guarantee the realization of its goals, and to accomplish interest rate target in the process. In China, things are a little different since the intermediate target of China's monetary policy is money aggregates rather than interest rate. Therefore the problem is whether the central bank could accomplish money aggregates target when it adopts an exchange rate regime similar to fixed ones, and imposes relatively strict capital control. The answer is yes. Similar to what has been previously mentioned, the central bank can withdraw currency to meet money aggregates target. But generally speaking, the central bank cannot accomplish interest rate target and money aggregates target simultaneously, that is to say, it cannot control money supply and interest rate at the same time. In reality, China does set deposit and loan interest rate target as well as money aggregates target. Are the two targets contradictory to each other? I believe, first, money aggregates target is namely set by the central bank, but in practice, the central bank has not strictly implemented the plan. From 2005 to 2010, the M_2 target was never met and the average absolute value of the deviation of the actual figure from the target stood around 2.5%. Second, money aggregates target is undergoing constant adjustment, making the accomplishment of both targets possible, since potential contradictions are taken into consideration when the targets are set. For example, M_2 target was set at 17% for 2010, while 16%, 14%, and 13% for the next three years. Third, different from benchmark deposit and loan interest rate, money aggregates target is not to impact the scale of deposits and loans. Therefore, it is possible for the central bank to control both targets.

SECTION THREE: TRANSFORMING INTERMEDIATE TARGETS — FROM QUANTITY-BASED TO PRICE-BASED

Since the central bank usually cannot realize these ultimate goals directly, it needs to use intermediate targets. So the intermediate targets of monetary policy refer to adjustable indicators between ultimate goals and variables directly operated by the central bank. Intermediate targets can be further divided into intermediate targets and operating targets. In general, intermediate targets are indicators that the central bank adjusts and uses to observe the attainability of ultimate goals; operating targets, also called short-term targets, are policy variables effectively operated by the central bank using monetary policy tools.

Yet in the Chinese monetary policy system, normally no distinction is made between intermediate targets and operating targets. The Chinese central bank monitors two indicators in daily operations — excess reserve ratio and interbank offered rate. But in the current Chinese financial market, these two indicators are not under the central bank's direct control. Rather, they are shaped by financial institutions' behaviors in the market, so they do not conform to the definition of operating targets. In my opinion, distinguishing between intermediate targets and operating targets does not have much practical meaning, so in this book, they are both called intermediate targets.

Next, I will first introduce the historic developments of intermediate targets in China, then elaborate why money supply is no longer suitable as an intermediate target, then discuss the limitations of price-based intermediate targets, and finally introduce the transformational concept of replacing quantity-based intermediate targets with price-based ones.

Historic Developments of Intersmediate Targets in China

The People's Bank of China began to assume the role of a central bank only in 1983. In contrast with western countries that have accumulated lots of experience managing monetary policies in the last century, the development of China's monetary policy targets has only a short history of about 30 years. During this time, there were some rather significant moments. As policy environment, economic environment and other elements changed at these moments, intermediate targets of the central bank were also adjusted a few times.

Before the mid-1990s, the central bank resorted to direct control, i.e., used aggregate credit and currency in circulation as intermediate targets of its monetary policy in order to allocate money for the national economic plan. Management by the central bank basically maintained some practices of planned economy. Each year, the central bank would make two plans, one for credits and one for currency in circulation. Both plans are restrictive. By directly controlling these two targets, the central bank managed and adjusted the economy, preventing inflation and promoting economic growth. This process is summarized as one in which the central bank draws credit plans and allocates funds to state-owned banks, who maintain with the central bank a borrowing/lending relationship and engage in interbank lending along with other financial institutions. After 1987, China's economic reform faced complexities such as the reform of commodity prices, the reform of enterprises and the delegation of power and concession of profits to state-owned enterprises. During this time, credit rationing of financial institutions was developed, marketization deepened and a mechanism of effective resource allocation was established step by step. In this period, the central bank controlled credits well and so mitigated the risks of overheated economy and inflation. But because of their planned nature, these intermediate targets inevitably led to an imbalanced allocation of money and resources among regions and industries. The direction of monetary policy changed all the time.

In the 1990s, with further development of the economic system, various financial institutions gradually replaced the old system that consisted solely of state-owned banks; the proportion of loan increment of financial institutions other than state-owned commercial banks in total loan increment rose from 22% in 1990 to 49% in 1996; security market, interbank market, bond market and swap market all started to grow, increasing their influence on domestic money supply. If the central bank continued to monitor the credit scale of state-owned banks and not the total money supply in the society, it could not obtain information pertaining to the actual total money supply in the society, therefore could not gain sufficient understanding of the macroeconomic conditions, and so could not realize the ultimate goals of its monetary policy. But cancelling the original intermediate targets meant that new intermediate targets needed to be established. So, the task of setting money supply as an intermediate target was put on the agenda.

In 1995, the first central bank law of China, *Law of the People's Republic of China on the People's Bank of China*, was passed, which assigns to the People's Bank of China the role of making and implementing the monetary policy. Also at this time, the PBOC tried to integrate money supply into the intermediate target system of its monetary policy. In 1996, the bank officially made money supply an intermediate target, announcing its 3 indicators, M_0, M_1, and M_2, which refer to cash in circulation, narrow money and broad money respectively. Currency in circulation thereby ceased to be an intermediate target. At the same time, because the share of loans in society's monetary liquidity decreased and the share of state-owned commercial banks' loan increment in total loan increment of all financial institutions dropped to 70% that year, credit plans alone also failed to reflect true liquidity in the economy. Therefore, aggregate credit began to be replaced as an indicator, too.

On December 24, 1997, the PBOC decided to lift the lending cap of state-owned commercial banks and to promote debt-to-asset ratio management and risk management, adopting a new management mechanism in which banks would be guided by the central bank's plan on loan increment, dispose funds in an independent and balanced way and closely monitor different ratios and the central bank would adopt an intermediate way of macroeconomic control. The People's Bank of China no longer issued quarterly mandatory lending plan to commercial banks, but issued instead annual (quarterly) guiding plan as a monitoring target of the central bank's macroeconomic control, providing reference for commercial banks when they drafted their own fund disposal plans.

In 1998, the People's Bank of China lifted its restriction on the credit scale of state-owned commercial banks, indicating the change from direct to indirect macro-financial control. The bank abandoned major prior ways of managing credit scale, and began to comprehensively adopt a series of monetary policy tools including open market operation, reserve ratio, rediscounting, relending, and interest rate to indirectly adjust money supply. Money supply truly became a major intermediate target of the central bank's monetary policy. Around this time, the central bank began to issue official base currency plans to determine base currency according to various factors like economic conditions, level of inflation and monetary liquidity in the society. And because aggregate credit is a controllable indicator connected relatively closely to money supply, the central bank included aggregate credit into its system of intermediate targets after lifting the control over credit scale.

From 1998 till now, new intermediate targets have basically been set. The central bank relies mainly on quantity-based indicator (money supply, chiefly M_2), uses credit scale as a guiding indicator, and combined currency issuing and interbank offered rate to form a system of intermediate targets, which demonstrates its monetary policy's feature of indirect control.

Why is Money Supply no Longer Suitable as Intermediate Target?

In general, intermediate targets of monetary policy can be divided into two types: price-based and quantity-based. Price-based intermediate targets consist mainly of interest rate and exchange rate, while quantity-based targets chiefly include money supply. These two types of targets correlate with price-based control and quantity-based control respectively. As mentioned before, China used to use money supply as an intermediate target and adopted a quantity-based control model. But as the economy embraces the "New Normal" and as interest rates are being marketized, the government and the market have reached consensus on transforming quantity-based control into price-based control. Drawing from international experience, central banks of major western countries usually adopt price-based operative indicators, which may vary according to each country's economic development. For example, the Federal Reserve chose the federal funds rate, the ECB chose the main refinancing rate, and the Bank of England chose the interest rate on 14-day Treasury bill repurchases.

There are three major standards when a central bank chooses intermediate targets: measurability, controllability and relevance. These three standards raise requirements of different levels for intermediate targets, which are as follows: The central bank can collect relatively accurate statistics on these variables chosen as intermediate targets of the monetary policy; the central bank can, with relatively high certainty, keep the chosen intermediate targets within a certain or expected range; and that the variables chosen as intermediate targets are closely related to the ultimate targets of monetary policy and are conducive to their realization.

As economic and financial conditions change, the shortcomings and limitations of M_2 as an intermediate target gradually begin to show, making the adoption of price-based targets increasingly urgent. As mentioned before, there are three standards for the selection of monetary policy's intermediate targets: measurability, controllability and relevance. During the rest of this section, I will analyze the pros and cons of price-based and quantity-based intermediate targets under the current environment of China with the help of these three standards. In the analysis, I will use Shibor as a potential choice for price-based intermediate target.

Measurability

Measurability means that the central bank can collect relatively accurate statistics on the intermediate targets. Because of the development of information technology and financial innovation, it is hard to define the scope of money supply as a concept. There will be omissions and mistakes in the traditional calculation of M_0, M_1, M_2, and M_3. And because China currently exerts complex control over commercial banks, many off-balance-sheet businesses and financial innovation products are not included in the calculation of M_2, undermining M_2's measurability and accuracy of calculation.

Now let us take a look at Shibor. Since its launch in 2007, a quoting group consisting of 18 banks gives daily interbank offered rates with maturities ranging from overnight, 1-week, 2-week, 1-month, 3-month, 6-month, 9-month to 1-year. The Shibor of all maturities is then calculated by arithmetically averaging all the quotations of the 18 banks, with the four highest and four lowest quotations excluded. Beginning from August 1, 2014, Shibor is published at 9:30 (previously at 11:30) on each business day. This move demonstrates the regulatory authority's intention of making Shibor the benchmark interest rate.

Controllability

Because money supply = monetary base × money multiplier, a central bank's control over money supply depends on its ability to control the monetary base and to predict the money multiplier. The central bank of China does not have much problem controlling the monetary base. In fact, as the central bank moves from passive control through funds outstanding for foreign exchange to active control through open market operations (or other similar tools), its control over the monetary base is becoming more accurate. However, the central bank does have severe problems predicting the money multiplier.

With regard to a central bank's control over money supply, the money multiplier is not under direct control of the bank. So the bank can predict only the multiplier, and adjust the scope of monetary base accordingly, so as to realize the goals of broad money supply. Yet money multiplier is influenced by very complex factors such as behavior of banks, wealth distribution among residents, financial innovation, etc., which are all independent to monetary policy operations of the central bank, therefore creating substantial difficulties for the bank to predict the multiplier.

Judging from the results, the Chinese central bank's control over M_2 is indeed unsatisfactory. Between 2004 and 2014, the standard deviation between actual amount of M_2 and targeted amount of M_2 was 3%. Excluding the figures from year 2009 which had the biggest deviation (over 10%), the figure of rest of the years still stood at 1.8%, indicating that there are indeed problems regarding the controllability of M_2.

If the central bank changes from quantity-based control to price-based control, international experience would show that central banks have very strong control over their benchmark interest rates. This is mainly because a central bank can indefinitely increase/decrease base money in the money market, making sure that the monetary base always reaches the bank's targeted level. For example, if the bank sets the target interest rate at 2% while the market interest rate is 4%, all that the bank needs to do is to increase base money until interest rate drops to 2%. Besides, because of a central bank's strong ability to intervene the money market interest rate, once it sets the target rate, the market will soon adjust interest rate to the targeted level, contributing to the realization of the bank's goal. Take the US as an example. After 2009, average standard deviation between money market interest rates and target interest rates was always within ±0.2%; between 2000 and 2006, that figure was within ±0.3%.

Relevancy

The relevancies between M_2 growth and real economy indicators (such as GDP and CPI growth rate) have weakened drastically over the past decade

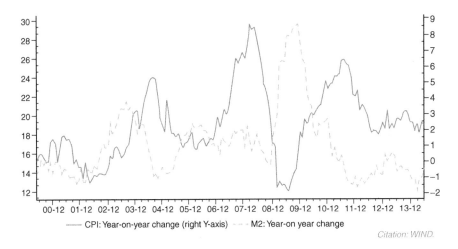

Figure 4.4 Year-on-year M_2 growth precedes year-on-year CPI growth by 2 years.

while the fluctuations of interest rate have been more volatile. The appropriateness of keeping using money supply as an intermediate target for China's monetary policy is under challenge, more so than ever.

The logic behind the central bank's choice of M_2 as an intermediate target is that under the currency circulation equation $MV = PV$, if the central bank controls money supply M, then it can control the aggregate production Y and price P; when the economy grows too fast and pressure of inflation rises, the bank can cool down the economy, meet the goals and control inflation by cutting down money supply.

History shows that adjusting and controlling inflation through M_2 is the most effective. Figure 4.4 shows that the excess M_2 growth leads to a CPI surge with a lag of one to two years; in response to rapid CPI growth, the central bank immediately cuts down money supply to prevent inflation surge. The most typical case took place from 2009 to 2011 when CPI kept rising and M_2 dropped from 30% to 12%. This was the central bank's reverse operation targeted at CPI.

In recent years, however, as capital use has been increasingly inefficient in China's financial system and the pace of currency circulation has also dropped, the relevancies between money supply and growth and inflation have weakened. Specifically, from the second half of 2012 to the first half of 2013, M_2 grew rapidly but little pressure was noticed on inflation as CPI fluctuated in a small range from 2% to 3%. Meanwhile, the growth rate of M_2 and that of GDP became more and more different and the fluctuation of M_2 imposed far less impact on GDP. All these indicate that the relevancies between money supply and the goals of monetary policy have weakened and become unstable. International experience shows that the opening-up of the financial sector changes the intermediate targets.

Furthermore, the year-on-year M_2 is basically equivalent to the year-on-year loan balance, reflecting the size of indirect financing in the banking system. When financial innovation booms, direct financing takes a bigger share, making indirect financing unable to present the real picture of financing. Therefore, Total Social Financing (TSF) was adopted. Starting from 2011, the central bank has been releasing TSF data as a supplement to money supply. TSF = RMB loans + foreign currency loans + entrusted loans + trust loans + bankers' acceptance (BA) + corporate bonds + non-financial institutions' equity sales + insurance claims + property investment by insurance companies + others.

However, controversy has long hovered around the "overlapping calculation" of TSF. Sheng Songcheng, Director-General of Financial Survey and Statistics Department of PBOC, said that there was no "overlapping" in the calculation of TSF. Take entrusted loans for example. Company A finances through corporate bonds and later loans the fund to company B through entrusted loans. The same fund will be calculated twice into TSF. Although the two loans use the same fund, they differ in risk and interest rate, which makes them two separate loans. That is why the fund, though calculated twice, still does not count as "overlapping calculation."

I agree with the above argument that there exists no "overlapping calculation." However, the example given above does justify that TSF as an indicator is irrelevant. If company A invests with the fund it has financed, it will directly generate GDP; if A lends the fund to B who uses it for investment, GDP grows by the same amount but through two financing activities. Comparing the two scenarios, TSF differs by one time while GDP grows by similar amounts. Due to the huge diversity in using raised money, TSF is plagued with low-efficient and even zero-efficient money usage, rendering it poorly relevant to the goals.

As to the relevancy with the interest rate target, no proper method exists in China for research. Since money supply is the major target, interest rate is in a passive position, reflecting the changes in money supply. It is impossible to separate the relation between interest rate and the goals from that between money supply and the goals.

Theoretically, interest rate and the goals are of reciprocal causation, namely, when inflation rises, the central bank raises interest rate, pushing down inflation; when inflation drops, the central bank cuts down interest rate. Statistics from the US and Australia show that prior to the 2008 financial crisis, such a reciprocal causation was significant. The results of adjusting and controlling show it is effective to meet the goals through interest rate adjustment. With the exception of the financial crisis, the US has maintained CPI between 1% and 4% and GDP growth between 1% and 5%; Australia has kept its CPI from 0 to 5% and GDP from 2% to 5%. In contrast, China's CPI has passed 5% for multiple times and dropped under −1%; the fluctuations of GDP are even more volatile.

As a reference for the pricing of financial products, the benchmark interest rate is one of the most important financial infrastructures for interest rate liberalization. As the control over interest rate loosens, to build and develop the benchmark interest rate for China's money market has become one of the most vital missions in promoting interest rate liberalization. In 2007, The Shanghai Interbank Offered Rate (Shibor) was established, the beginning of the all-round efforts to build the benchmark interest rate for China's money market. So far, Shibor has established itself as the benchmark interest rate, playing a key role in the pricing of marketized financial products and the pricing inside and outside commercial banks.

A Comparison Between Quantity-Based Adjustment and Price-Based Adjustment

In general, quantitative adjustment and price adjustment are not that different given the "linear duality" between the quantity and price of money, namely, the increase in money supply usually leads to interest rate decline.

However, as discussed in the first chapter, due to the difference in the injection of base money, the relation between the quantity and the price is unstable. Different targets for base money injection create different effects to interest rate. When the increase of funds outstanding for foreign reserves is mostly passive, it becomes more difficult to control the benchmark rate. It is because the central bank can only withdraw money through the money market, namely, raising the interest rate in the money market instead of cutting it. As a result, the overall amount of money injection stays the same — the money is withdrawn from the money market and injected into other markets. The conditions for price-based adjustment are immature. As RMB rate enters the equivalent zone, the channels for base money injection change, making price-based adjustment a possibility. Meanwhile, quantity-based adjustment and price-based adjustment are difficult to tell apart. For instance, the central bank adjusts base money injection through open market operations to control the benchmark interest rate. Such an adjustment can be defined as both quantity-based and price-based.

Generally speaking, price-based adjustment is more effective when mostly carried out through property prices, which better suits the adjustment demands in the financial innovation boom. Nevertheless, price-based adjustment has two defects: first, the "liquidity trap" or "zero lower bound," namely, when the interest rate is targeted at 0%, it is almost impossible to exert monetary control by lowering interest rate; second, interest adjustment is a general policy rather than a structural one; quantity-based adjustment tools are directional. For example, in QE, treasury bonds and mortgage-backed securities (MBS) of certain maturity were purchased to support certain assets and financial products of certain maturity.

China, now at a critical stage of structural reform, is not up to comprehensive interest rate adjustment. Therefore, quantity-based goals will still be important for a long time. On the one hand, support is demanded from relevant government authorities to facilitate the transformation; on the other hand, financing should be restricted when soft intervention, ineffective risk pricing, overcapacity or "zombie companies" are involved. In conclusion, quantity-based adjustment will stay in the picture for a long time to come.

Orientation in the Intermediate Targets Transformation

PBOC and IMF, in a Beijing seminar held in March 2014, discussed the new issues in monetary policy. Ma Jun, Chief Economist of PBOC, argues that the China's monetary policy should turn to policy interest rate as an intermediate target. He has put forward a new framework for monetary policy: in the short term a policy interest rate (as an intermediate target) should be maintained and in the medium- to long-term, M_3 growth should be referred to as an indicator. Under this framework, the main objective in the short term is to keep the policy interest rate within the predetermined target range instead of stabilizing all the quantitative indicators (such as certain average movement of M_3 growth), which can only be policy reference in the mid- to long-term.

Ma argues that it will take China two to three years to transform from quantity-based intermediate targets to the new framework. He has also proposed a possible roadmap. First, building a *de facto* interest rate corridor around the implicit policy rate with no need to announce it. Such a corridor can help mitigate interest rate volatility given a constant average rate. Second, narrowing down the *de facto* interest rate corridor. Third, when abolishing the benchmark interest rate, PBOC should in the meantime announce to establish a new policy framework featuring short-term policy interest rate and medium- to long-term M_3 growth reference. When conditions permit, an official corridor could be set up where the upper limit is the interest rate of the Standing Lending Facility (SLF) and the lower limit the interest rate of the excess reserves. In the official corridor, open market operations will still be used to maintain a narrower *de facto* corridor.

I think this roadmap is feasible but further research is required to determine the intermediate target. So far, the central bank is more confident about the control over the medium-term interest rate, which is the 3.5% interest rate for the Medium-term Lending Facility (MLF). As for the short-term interest rate in the money market, the bank tends to follow the market with the repo and reverse repo rates fluctuating along the market rate. Nevertheless, since the explicit short-term interest rate is plagued with grave moral hazard, such a situation will continue for a considerably long time. As a result, the transition period will witness multiple intermediate targets of "mitigating short-term interest rate volatility + stabilizing medium-term interest rate + directional adjustment of financing scale" and give equal weight to quantity-based and price-based adjustments. In the long run, the possible benchmark rate may consist of Shibor, Loan Prime Rate (LPR) and return rate of 10-year government bonds, which are respectively referred to as short-term, medium-term and long-term benchmark rate. As the financial market grows, the short-term interest rate — Shibor — will play an increasingly important role.

Chapter Five
New Monetary Policy Tools

This chapter focuses on three kinds of new monetary policy tools — targeted monetary policy tools, interest rate corridor and expectations management. Targeted monetary policy tools refer to targeted reserve requirement ratio cuts, targeted re-lending and so on, which have been used by the central bank in 2014. Interest rate corridor monetary policy tools refer to Standing Lending Facility and (SLF) and so on, the basis of interest rate corridor in China. Expectations management refers to the central bank guiding the public expectation by releasing information to achieve monetary policy targets at a low cost.

SECTION ONE: TARGETED MONETARY POLICY TOOLS

In 2015, under the overall declining economy, the People's Bank of China began to launch structural monetary policy tools. Structural monetary policy tools, a part of the unconventional monetary policy, generally refer to linking money supply with specific structural targets. In this year, in order to achieve the overall target of reducing social financing cost, the central bank linked credit increment ratio of medium, small and micro-sized enterprises with base money releasing. However, this policy did not work. The weighted average interest rate and the rising loan interest rates proportion increased in 2014, among which the general loan interest rate climbed from 7.14% at the end of 2014 to 7.33%.

Structural monetary policy tools did not originate from China. Instead, the developed countries are the pioneers in structural monetary policy tools, such as the Quantitative Easing (QE) in the US, Funding for Lending Scheme (FLS) in Britain and Targeted Long-term Refinancing Operations (TLTRO) in Europe, all of which aim to lower systematic risk or to push commercial banks to expand credit and loan to speed up economic recovery. As the structural monetary policy is first used after financial crisis, it is usually considered by investors as the policy to help crisis rescue and economic recovery. But in nature, it does not have to be crisis disposal policies. It is an innovation jointly promoted by the global central bank, to bring a new page of monetary policy.

Both US and Europe launched the QE policy after the financial crisis, but with different purposes. Thus, structural monetary policy is flexible and changeable, and can be used for various targets. As to the QE policy in the United States, the Federal Reserve bought $1.725 trillion of agency debt and mortgage-backed securities in the first round QE (QE1). In the second and third rounds (QE2 and QE3), the Federal Reserve turned to Treasury bonds and mortgage-backed securities. We can see that the real estate market stimulation to avoid balance-sheet shrink brought by declining real estate has always been the focus of the United States. As the liquidity risk of financial institutions in the early phase faded away, the Federal Reserve turned to lower long-term interest rate to speed up economic recovery. But in Europe, the most severe problem is the European sovereign debt crisis. The soaring sovereign debt risk in European peripheral countries, especially in Greece, is the most important reason for the launching of the QE policy.

From the experience of other countries, the stimulative monetary policy worked effectively. The US recovered from the financial crisis through the QE policy. Japan had been carrying out ultralow interest rate policy since 2008, but was still stuck in depression. From when the QE policy aiming at raising inflation started in April 2013, the economy in Japan has begun to recover. At the same time, the Japanese central bank kept buying high risk Stock Fund, Exchange Traded Fund and Real Estate

Investment Trust in its QE policy, bringing a booming stock market in Japan. Thus, structural monetary policy tools overcome the balance sheet crisis and persistent deflation, both of which are the weakness of traditional policy. And targeted at the risky and vulnerable sectors of the economy, these tools tend to the recovery of economy.

As for China, it is time to use structural monetary policy tools. At present, China's economic growth momentum has begun to switch from investment to consumption. The sluggish "three carriages" — investment, consumption and export — lead to the declining economy. As the traditional monetary policy is either tight or loose, it is unable to tackle the economy growth and the structure adjustment at the same time. In order to avoid the structural unemployment and overstimulation to overcapacity industries, China has no choice to take advantage of structural monetary policy. This is the reason structural monetary policy was introduced in 2014. Since 2013, the central bank has introduced several kinds of structural monetary policy tools. Medium-term Lending Facility (MLF), with the general duration of three months, rolling over many times and should be pledged with eligible collaterals. In 2014, the central bank provided MLF to those financial institutions that expand loans to rural areas and small enterprises as required. Meanwhile, if the financial institutions meet the standard, the central bank cannot refuse to release money. Thus MLF has strong stimulating effect on financial institutions. The main function of the SLF is to meet the liquidity demand of long period and large amount of financial institutions. It also should be pledged with eligible collaterals, provided on demand and become the basis of interest rate corridor. In 2014, the central bank decided whether to provide SLF or not and the scale of SLF according to market. Pledged Supplementary Lending (PSL), similar to MLF, with longer duration, is a medium-term policy tool to promote long-term investments. In 2014, the central bank provided PSL to policy banks. The structural monetary policy tools introduced in 2013 also include Short-term Liquidity Operations (SLOs) and re-lending to the rural and small enterprises.

In conclusion, the structural monetary policy tools in China include three types: liquidity management tools, supporting the rural and small enterprises tools and investment support tools. These enable the central bank to adjust support on investment and real economy according to the demand of economic growth and structure adjustment, so as to achieve the two goals flexibly.

Does structural monetary policy have effect only on economic downturn? Can it solve the problem of overheating economy? I think the answer is yes. The meaning of structural monetary policy lies in the close link between monetary base and bank lending. So structural monetary policy can still play a role in crunching some overheating industries and risky fields. For instance, by adjusting the support weight of some industries in base money releasing, the central bank can raise the support cost of commercial banks, realizing the industry crunch without hurting other industries.

We talked about the advantages of structural monetary policy above. But is structural monetary policy so perfect? Certainly not. In fact, there are great difficulties in carrying out structural monetary policy. First of all, the biggest drawback of structural monetary policy is the unclear ultimate goal. For example, in Britain, after FLS, capital flowed to real estate industry, boosting the overall housing price, and the central bank was to blame. In China, the structural monetary policy in 2014 caused capital flow to the bond market and the note market, bringing the bull bond market. The money of banks will automatically flow into the sectors of high return but low risk and the lack of observation target will lead to the failure of structural monetary policy. Second, structural monetary policy faces difficulties in solving the banks' reluctance to lend, as well as overheating in certain industries. Risk aversion leads banks to be reluctant to lend. In China, the bad debt increased sharply in 2014, resulting in tight credit. Under this circumstance, the low interest rate policy failed to encourage banks to lend, and the banks still prevented small enterprises which were exposed to risk constantly from credit. As for the overheating problem, structural monetary policy is unable to curb the investment impulse of commercial banks. Last, in a usual situation that is not a crisis, structural monetary policy may cause structural distortion. If the measures taken are not in accordance with the rule of market operation, the policy is interfering with the economy operation, bringing negative effects on the real economy.

In conclusion, I think structural monetary policy tools have many advantages, working more effectively in structural adjustment, risk prevention and targeted stimulation than traditional policy. But they also have some disadvantages, such as unclear goals, failure in solving tight lending of banks and overheating economy, and structural distortion. The priority is to establish an appropriate appraisal system to help structural monetary policy play its role.

SECTION TWO: INTEREST RATE CORRIDOR MONETARY POLICY TOOLS

The traditional monetary policy tools are the general tools used by central banks around the world, focusing on serving the real economy. The central bank decided the specific quantity and direction of operation according to the economic growth and general price signals. Especially, the reserve requirement ratio and the rediscount rate show the obvious cyclical characteristic. With the increasingly complex economic operation and changing external environment, whether such toolbox can meet the needs of the central bank to play different roles has become the urgent problem calling for attention.

First, after the subprime crisis, in China, influenced by the increasing uncertainty in international economy and the fluctuating liquidity factors, the volatility of the supply and demand of short-term liquidity in the banking system also increased. Especially when multiple factors are working together or the market expectation is changing, it is likely that the gap between short-term capital supply and demand cannot be eliminated by financing from money market, not only increasing the difficulty in liquidity management for financial institutions, but also bad for the liquidity adjustment of the central bank.

Second, in 2011 and 2012, the real economy had strong demand for capital, which was not covered by banks due to the limitation on credit scale and capital adequacy ratio. In the situation of adequate liquidity in the interbank market, financial institutions considered interbank market as the main source of cheap capital, ignoring the stable retail customers. Interbank borrowing took an increasing proportion in the liability of the banking system. The proportion of interbank non-standard assets in total assets of some banks was far more than the international average level. Thus, serious liquidity risk was accumulated in the banking system. Once liquidity squeeze appears in the interbank market, some banks are likely to repeat the bank run crisis that happened in Britain Northern Rock Bank.

Third, the open market operation providing liquidity support to interbank market has many defects. The first one is that it is not timely enough. The routine open market operation always inquires on Monday and Wednesday, and operates on Tuesday and Thursday. If the liquidity squeeze happens in the non-operating days, open market operation can do nothing about it. The second problem is the too narrow objects. The objects of open market operation are the primary dealers in interbank market. In 2012, there were only 49 primary dealers, including 42 commercial banks, 6 securities companies and one insurance company. The central bank pumps in liquidity through the primary dealers, which makes it difficult and uncertain for the non-primary dealers to get money. The third one is the high technical requirement. The routine open market operation is executed by the financial markets department at the People's Bank of China, through the system of integrated service platform. But the financial institutions in rural areas, such as city commercial banks, rural commercial banks, rural cooperative banks and so on, lack the support system. It is technically difficult for them to get liquidity even if the central bank pumps in liquidity.

Therefore, it is necessary to innovate and improve the liquidity supply and adjustment mechanism so as to promote the liquidity management of commercial banks and prevent liquidity risk in the banking system. Globally, both in developed and developing countries, the central banks are equipped with this kind of emergency tool to prevent short-term liquidity shock, such as Discount Window in the US, Marginal Lending Facility in Europe, Complementary Lending Facility in Japan, Operational Standing Facility in Britain, Standing Liquidity Facility in Canada, Liquidity Adjustment Loans in Singapore, Collateralized Lending in Malaysia and Secured Loans in Russia.

In early 2013, the People's Bank of China introduced two tools, SLF and SLO. They are the emergency liquidity supply channels besides the routine open market operation, to meet the financial institutions' demand for long period and large amount liquidity support. The policy objects at the very start were policy banks and national commercial banks and the duration is one to three months. The interest rates are decided according to the need of policy regulating and guiding market rates. SLF should be pledged, with the eligible collaterals including high credit rating bond assets and high-quality credit assets. In January 2014, the objects were further expanded to pilot institutions in Beijing, Jiangsu, Shandong, Guangdong, Hebei, Shanxi, Zhejiang, Jilin, Henan, and Shenzhen. The local branch institutions of the PBC provides short-term liquidity support to those small and medium-sized financial institutions that meet the requirements. In June and spring festival period in 2013, the central bank took similar measures to deal with the abnormal liquidity fluctuation. From June to September in 2013, the balance of SLF was 416 billion, 396 billion, 410 billion and 386 billion respectively.

SLOs are mainly Reverse REPO within seven days, can be extended in case of holiday, and adopt the market-oriented interest rates bid method. The central bank decides the timing, scale and the term of operation according to the liquidity in interbank market and money market rates. This tool, in principle, is used at the intermittent period of routine open market operation. The policy objects are primary dealers in open market business who are systemically important, with good assets condition and work effectively in policy transmission. And the operation result will be disclosed in Announcement of Open Market Business a month later.

SLO and SLF have significant meaning in guiding public expectation, stabilizing the market, improving the regulation effects on money market rates and enhancing the central bank's ability to deal with sudden liquidity fluctuations.

First, SLO and SLF suggest the trend of open market operation to have a reasonable upper and lower bound. After Prime Minister Li Keqiang put floor and ceiling on economic growth, the open market operation of the central bank tends to adopt the interest rate corridor model, with the ceiling that will not cause systematic financial risk nor hurt real economy, and the floor that will not encourage term mismatch and over-leverage, as well as the real estate bubble.

Second, SLO and SLF help to stabilize the money market rates. As the necessary complements to routine open market operations, SLO and SLF are discretionarily used when interbank market liquidity fluctuates, playing a positive role for the stability of money market rates.

What is more, the launch of SLO and SLF further improve the liquidity management system of the central bank. Previously, the liquidity management tools include the bill, deposit reserve, repurchase and so on, lacking the shorter term liquidity management tool. As market interest rates fluctuate wildly during holidays, the importance of the term liquidity management tool is quite prominent. After the launch of SLO and SLF, the central bank has the short-term, medium-term and long-term liquidity management tools, more capable of restraining the high volatility of the short-term money market rates.

Last, the launch of SLO and SLF helps the central bank to improve the benchmark interest rate system, SHIBOR, Loan Prime Rate and Treasury Bonds Yield. SLO and SLF may gradually share the signal function of benchmark interest rates, and become the monetary policy targets. SLF and other open market operations focus on money market rates such as SHIBOR, while deposit reserve ratio is for long-term interest rates such as Loan Prime Rate.

Although China's interest rate corridor monetary policy tools are similar to European tools, there are still great differences. In Europe, financial institutions are active while the central bank is passive in the use of interest rate corridor. The central bank sets the target range of interest rate, then plays the role of market maker, rather than take the initiative to participate in the market. On the contrary, except some moments of extreme liquidity squeeze, MLF and other tools are controlled by the central bank. The central bank decides the objects, scale and interest rate of these tools, and does not publish to the public. Thus, to some extent, China's interest rate corridor monetary policy tools are non-market-oriented. Under the foreign exchange outflows and the great liquidity gap in market, interest rate corridor monetary policy tools are too opaque and unfair to take the role as the main channel of releasing base money, and the traditional monetary policy tools such as reserve requirement ratio are still very useful.

SECTION THREE: EXPECTATION MANAGEMENT MONETARY POLICY TOOLS

Expectation management methods can be divided into the traditional method and the modern method. Traditional expectation management method belongs to the instrumental variable method, that is, the government directly guides public expectation by manipulating policy tools. For example, the government affects expectations by changing interest rates. It is worth noting that the traditional method can only change expectations but not establish expectations, and may also bring serious side effects. For instance, austerity policy helps to lower public inflation expectation, but may also lead to serious economic recession. The modern expectation management method belongs to the strategy management method, that is, the government releases information to the public through various channels, guides and establishes public expectation by providing information fully and efficiently.

In expectation management, the central bank uses the traditional and modern methods comprehensively to improve public understanding of macroeconomic policy, improve the accuracy of public expectations, guide, coordinate and stabilize public expectations, so as to minimize the side effects and maximize the policy effects. In expectation management, the most important is inflation expectation management. Inflation expectation is a subjective estimate about the direction and the amount of variation of inflation in future.

The stability of inflation expectation has significant influence on macroeconomy.

First of all, inflation expectation is one of the important determinants of the real inflation. Market experience suggests that inflation expectation will influence the general inflation from both the demand and supply sides. The high inflation era in the 1970s is the typical example of failure in expectation management while the moderate inflation era in the 1980s is the success of expectation management. Under the relatively stable public expectation, the sudden price shock will not affect the long-term investment, consumption and saving; the short-term price will return to the long-term equilibrium level quickly, easing the resource allocation distortion brought by inflation and playing the role of market price signal.

Second, after the financial crisis in 2008, inflation expectation became an important factor of monetary policy transmission. Expectation transmission is where the central bank conveys its policy ideas by open market operation and communication with commercial banks. For example, the intention to keep tight or loose monetary policy will be reflected in the central bank's adjustment on short-term interest rates, as well as promise on long-term interest rates. Receiving such signal, market participants will take the initiative to adjust their investment and consumption behavior. Despite the time lag in traditional monetary transmission mechanism, the expectation transmission channel can reflect the monetary policy intention at sight on the long-term goals of economic growth and inflation rate quickly, and stabilize the economy before great fluctuation.

Last, the change of inflation expectation actually reflects the credibility of monetary policy. The more stable the expectation is, the more credible will be the monetary policy. If the central bank adjusts the inflation expectation continuously, it suggests that the long-term inflation target cannot be realized. Setting a long-term, stable inflation target is an important content of expectation management.

All countries around the world attach great importance to inflation expectation management, taking the following measures. The first is inflation targeting, to improve public's confidence in controlling inflation through monetary policies. The second is public communication, to improve the monetary policy transparency and guide public expectation. The third is necessary limit on price of basic production factors, such as ensuring the guaranteed wage growth rate lower than the growth of productivity, to avoid wage–price spiral.

The Federal Reserve manages expectation through "forward-looking guidance." By defining policy tools clearly, explaining the conditions of adjusting policy, holding regular Federal Open Market Committee (FOMC) meetings and publishing the minutes of the meeting, the Federal Reserve makes the policy transparent and predictable to some extent so as to guide public expectation effectively. For example, after the financial crisis, the Federal Reserve declared to keep low interest rates until unemployment rate is markedly improved. Besides, it pointed inflation rate, employment rate and capacity utilization as the three conditions to adjust policy. FOMC repeatedly mentioned in its routine press release the duration of low interest rates. It declared that the low interest rate will last for a long time, QE policy will exit at a fathomable pace and there is no simple policy exit point but according to the unemployment rate and inflation rate. These guidelines have great effect on investors' behavior and the central bank no longer adjusts economy only by monetary policy tools.

The central bank of Japan started the low interest rate policy in 1991 and promised to keep zero rate policy until the deflation risk disappeared. Coordinating with other fiscal policies, Japan's economic situation has been improved. However, the burst of Internet bubble in the autumn of 2000 dragged the global economy slowdown, also deteriorated deflation in Japan. In order to prevent the economic recession and curb the deflation expectation, the central bank of Japan launched QE monetary policy officially in early 2001. As the previous policies had lowered the market interest rate to zero, the conventional monetary policy did not work. Thus, the central bank of Japan launched the new expectation management tool, namely the balance sheet of the central bank. This QE policy includes three aspects. The first one is the central bank promising to provide liquidity to the market continuously, until Consumer Price Index (CPI) is stable at the level of non-negative. The central bank hopes to generate inflation expectation through promising and to drive the real economy out of deflation. The second is changing the monetary policy intermediate targets. The central bank changed the operation targets from overnight interest rate to the balance of current account of deposit financial institutions. The third is the central bank outstanding central bank bills to buy long-term Treasury bonds held by financial institutions. At the exit of QE policy in 2006, the economy of Japan had already been out of the haze of deflation. Abenomics also takes advantage of expectation management to regulate and control economy. For instance, it was decided in the monetary policy meeting of Japan that the central bank would spare no effect to realize the goal of CPI rising 2% in two years. In fact, after Mr. Abe came to power, the central bank was once more asked to set the inflation target of 2% so as to boost the public expectation of higher inflation.

At present, the People's Bank of China still has doubts about expectation management. First, whether it is necessary to conduct expectation management. Second, whether there are any side effects of expectation management.

It is thought that it is unnecessary for China to conduct expectation management. Expectation management is more necessary when the traditional monetary policy tools fail. But at present, the traditional tools still work in China. So whether to conduct expectation management depends on the actual situation of economy.

Expectation management also has its weakness. First of all, there exists the cost of the central bank explaining to the public. We should take the possibility of misunderstanding and over-interpretation into account. Second, expectation management means that the central bank makes some promises, but once the situation changes, the central bank cannot operate in accordance with the stated goal and the promises cannot be realized, which will damage the credibility of the central bank. Third, expectation management calls for clear goals. While China, in transition period, with complicated factors, provides government expectations on economic growth and inflation, it cannot provide market expectations on interest rates. Otherwise, it may lead to over-leverage and moral hazards in financial institutions.

Despite the disagreement on comprehensive expectation management in China, there is no dispute about expectation management on inflation and other fundamental factors. The quarterly monetary policy report issued by the central bank plays an important role in expectation management. For example, in the monetary policy implementation report in the third quarter of 2014, the fifth part, monetary policy trends, first introduces China's macroeconomic outlook, then explains about the main policy ideas in the next stage. Each report will become the hotspots in market. With the transformation of the monetary policy and the development of financial market, expectation management will exert a growing important effect.

Chapter Six

New Transmission Mechanism for Monetary Policy

Monetary policy transmission mechanism refers to the process where monetary policies are realized with monetary policy tools. Research on the transmission mechanism focuses on interest rate channel, asset price channel, credit channel, etc. However, these channels do not represent the whole monetary policy transmission mechanism but form one of the many parts of the mechanism — how activities in the financial market (including interest rate, exchange rate, stock price, credit, etc.) impact the real economy. Nevertheless, researches on how central bank's monetary policies transmit into the financial market are scarce.

In the New Normal, China will build a "central bank → money market (benchmark interest rate) → financial market → real economy" transmission mechanism. In this mechanism, the process of "central bank → money market (benchmark interest rate)" mainly relies on short- to medium-term monetary tools such as open market operations and MLF; "money market (benchmark interest rate) → financial market" refers to the transmission from the money market to other markets; "financial market → real economy" stands for the traditionally defined monetary policy transmission channels.

The first section will discuss how the central bank adjusts the money market through base money injection; the second and third will focus on the transmission from the money market to the rest of the financial market by learning from international and domestic experience; in the last section I will put forward an analysis framework for the bond market based on the "Revised Taylor's Rule."

SECTION ONE: "CENTRAL BANK → MONEY MARKET" TRANSMISSION MECHANISM

Money market is for assets involved in short-term borrowing, lending, buying and selling with original maturities of one year or less, including the interbank lending market, the bill market, the Negotiable Certificate of Deposit (CD) market, the Treasury bill market, the credit market and the repo market. Interbank money market is an Over-the-Counter (OTC) market where organization investors trade large volumes of money. Since the volume, price and delivery are decided through negotiation between the two traders, this market could better suit organization investors' diversified demand for trading. This is why the interbank market has dominated the market structure of each and every country in the world.

The central bank's control over the money market is the first step toward the price-based adjustment, key in the money policy transmission mechanism. It should be noted that China used to pursue the quantity-based adjustment where the "money market" was not under the direct control of the central bank and was only subject to indirect impact of other monetary policies. In the following passages, I will first introduce how central banks manage the money market before moving on to the determinants in China's money market interest rate.

Money Market Interest Rate Adjustment Mechanism in Foreign Economies

The world has two major models for adjusting interest rate in the money market: open market operations model in the US and the interest rate corridor model in the EU. Since the interest rate in the money market is the benchmark interest rate for central banks' monetary policy, the two models correspond to two types of interest rate liberalization.

In the open market operation model, the Federal Open Market Committee (FOMC) is the decision maker. Under the Federal Reserve Act (1913), the Fed formulates monetary policies. The Fed has three main tools at its disposal to influence monetary policy: open market operations, discount rate and reserve requirement. The Board of Governors oversees the setting of the discount rate and reserve requirements while FOMC runs open market operations. The chair of the Board of Governors is also the chair of FOMC. By using the three tools, the Fed influences the depository institutions' money supply to and demand from the Federal Reserve banks and further changes the Federal funds rate. The Federal funds rate is the interest rate that banks charge each other for overnight loans of federal funds, which are the reserves held by banks at the Fed. The change in the rate may cause a series of chain effects, possibly spilling over to other short-term interest rates, exchange rate, long-term interest rates, the amount of money and loans. It will ultimately affect a range of economic indicators (such as employment, production, goods and service prices). Committee membership changes at the first regularly scheduled meeting of the year. Open market operations are carried out by the Domestic Trading Desk of the Federal Reserve Bank of New York under direction from the FOMC. The securities authorized by the Fed are limited to BA, government securities, and securities of government agencies, mainly short-term government bonds.

Under this model, the Fed changes the base money through open market operations such as selling and redeeming US government securities. For instance, if the Fed wants to raise the Federal funds rate (the US interbank-offered rate), it will sell government securities (usually Treasury bills) to withdraw base money. Selling T-bills will push down the T-bill price and push up the return rate. In this way, the monetary supply drops, and the yield of T-bills rises, both lifting the interest rate.

In the interest rate corridor model, the central bank provides interest rate facilities to financial institutions such as commercial banks to stabilize the interbank overnight interest rate within the target range. The ceiling of the corridor is the discount rate or the re-lending rate at which commercial banks could borrow from the central bank; the floor is the interest rate on excess reserves at which commercial banks could charge

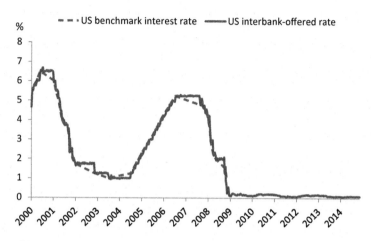

Figure 6.1   US interbank-offered rate and the benchmark interest rate are highly consistent. (Citation: WIND).

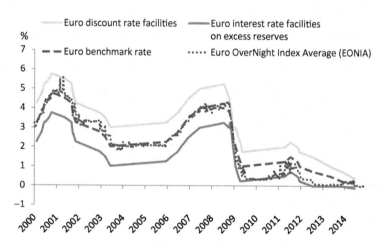

Figure 6.2   Euro OverNight Index Average (EONIA) is between the ceiling and floor of the interest rate corridor but deviates from the benchmark rate. (Citation: WIND)

for the excess reserves they put in the central bank. The short-term market interest rate can only fluctuate under the ceiling and above the floor. If it goes beyond the ceiling, commercial banks could borrow from the central bank at the ceiling rate and pull the market rate down back to the ceiling; if it goes under the floor, commercial banks will choose to put money into the central bank instead of offering it to other banks, pushing the market interest rate up to the floor.

In the EU interest rate corridor, the central bank sets the overnight interest rates for deposits and loans and the benchmark interest for loans (the ceiling being the deposit facility interest rate and the floor being the interest rate for marginal lending facility) for commercial banks. When the central bank wants to lower the interest rate, it will increase commercial banks' cost of lending from the central bank by lowering the interest rate for interbank overnight deposits and loans. Due to the lower cost, commercial banks are more willing to borrow from the central bank than from the money market, pushing down their interest rate in the money market.

Compared with the open market operation model, the interest corridor has several merits. First, it does not require a sophisticated government bond market. Open market operation, the activity of selling and buying of government bonds by the central bank, can only adjust the interest rate when both the central bank and the market hold a considerable amount of government bonds, whereas the interest rate corridor, involving no government bonds, only requires a sufficient amount of collaterals. Second, it costs less to manage the interest rate corridor as the purchase and sale of government bonds add more transaction costs to the central bank. In a large transaction, the central bank may suffer huge losses. In contrast, the yield of the interest rate corridor model is relatively stable. In fact, the central bank lends at a higher interest rate than it borrows, leaving little possibility for a loss.

The interest rate corridor also has defects. It can only adjust the short-term interest rate but not the long-term rate. In the open market operation model, the central bank can buy and sell government bonds of a specific maturity to change the maturity structure of interest rate. In the interest corridor model, however, additional long-term interest tools are demanded. This is why apart from the interest rate corridor, the ECB also uses Main Re-financing Operations (MROs) to adjust the medium-term interest rate.

It should be noted that when the interest rate is the direct target, interest rate in the money market sees little fluctuation and interest rates of maturities less than one year (overnight, seven-day, one-month, and six-month) come close. This is because with price-based adjustment money market, interest rate is no longer an independent variant. The central bank has to maintain a certain target interest rate for a prolonged period of time, which leads to stable expectations for the interest rate in one year. As a result, the maturity premium within a year is zero. In contrast, the interest rates on overnight, seven-day, one-month, and six-month borrowing keep rising.

Determinants of China's Money Market Interest Rate

China's money market is not under the direct control of the central bank but is the mediate target of the bank's monetary policy. So the market is secondary in the monetary policy system. In the meantime, since quantity-based adjustment used to prevail in China, money was injected passively through funds outstanding for foreign exchange, different from the active injection under the price-based adjustment. In the old model, the central bank managed to control base money injection by managing the scale of foreign exchange purchase, but the process is different from that in the US and the EU.

Under the Federal funds interest rate model, what the Fed changes is the amount of excess reserve whereas in the EU interest rate corridor, the ECB changes the monetary base in the overnight market. In China, where money is injected through funds outstanding for foreign exchanges, the central bank changes the monetary in the whole nation. In the US and EU, base money injection is mostly short-term and targeted at banks and therefore directly impacts the interest rate for short-term financing. In China, however, as base money injection with indefinite terms targets corporations, households and foreign investors, it is unable to influence the short-term interest rate.

The question now is: what determines the interest rate in China's money market?

We can see from Figure 6.3 that prior to 2013, the interest rate in China's money market was virtually determined by inflation alone; even after 2013, the changes in interest rate are in line with those in inflation. It is simply because the central bank continues to target inflation through its monetary policy. The section "Should the Central Bank be Independent" has already discussed this issue as follows: the four-goal system is only

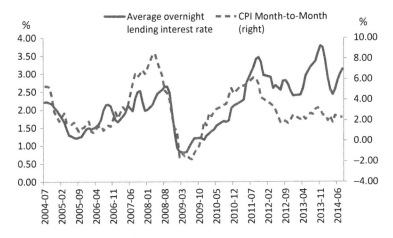

Figure 6.3   Inflation determines the interest rate in China's money market. (Citation: WIND)

nominal as inflation usually outweighs other indicators and dominates the bank's monetary policy with a handful of exceptions. Specifically, the central bank influences the overall interest rate in the financial system by changing the benchmark deposit and lending interest rate, the reserve ratio, the scale and price of open market operation, all on the basis of inflation. The money market interest rate, being the most sensitive, will no doubt respond to the above changes. What happened in 2011 is the most typical. The economy began to go down in the second half of 2010 with GDP and industrial added value sliding to the level in 2009 and 2007 respectively. The central bank, which targeted at inflation rather than growth, lifted reserve rate and interest rate to tackle high inflation, causing a surge in the money market interest rate in 2011.

The interest rate in China's money market determined independently by financial institutions is free from the direct control of the central bank (except verbal intervention) and the bank has no definite target interest rate. The resulting uncertainty in financial institutions' expectations of the interest rate leads to the stratification in the interest rates of different maturities. For example, in 2014, the average overnight lending interest rate was around 2.8%, the average seven-day rate 3.5%, the average one-month repo interest rate 4.2% and the average six-month repo interest rate

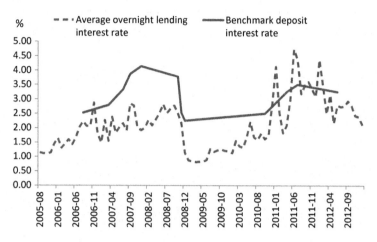

Figure 6.4 Interest rate in the money market is closely linked to the benchmark deposit and lending interest rate. (Citation: WIND)

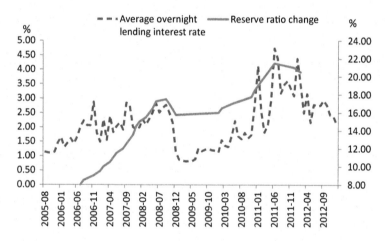

Figure 6.5 Money market interest rate and the reserve ratio change in the same direction. (Citation: WIND)

4.8%. This is highly different from countries that choose the money market interest as the target rate, where interest rates of all maturities tend to be close.

As a result, the interest rate in China's money market is unsuitable to be the benchmark rate, as being a benchmark rate requires small fluctuation and little change. Notwithstanding, in the following sections, I will still use the money market interest rate as the benchmark to study its interaction with other interest rates. However, when we are looking at the bond market, we must set aside the money market interest rate, which will be elaborated in the fifth section.

Section Two: "Money Market → Bond Market" Transmission Mechanism

China's bond market can be largely divided into government bonds, debenture bonds and convertible bonds. Convertible bonds are more like stocks than bonds, thus bearing huge difference from bonds in a traditional sense. Government bonds carry no credit risks while debenture bonds do, thus the yield of the latter is higher than that of the former of the same term, and the difference between the two is credit spread. Domestically or internationally, the market has basically achieved a consensus on the pricing of bond yield, which is:

Yield of government bond = Benchmark interest rate + Term spread
Yield of debenture bond = Benchmark interest rate + Term spread
+ credit spread.

The money market rate is usually considered as the benchmark interest rate. Next, I will elaborate on the "benchmark interest rate → short-term government bonds" and the "short-term government bond → long-term government bond" transmission mechanisms. Section Five will present the complete bond market analysis framework without considering benchmark interest rate and also the determinants of credit spread that are unique to China.

International Experience on the Transmission Mechanism from Money Market to Short-Term Government Bonds

Government bonds mainly include Treasury and the financial bonds issued by the three policy banks. In addition, central bank bills, local government debts, and railway bonds fall into the category of government bond by certain measures. The spread between different kinds of government bonds is mainly determined by tax premium (Treasury bonds are tax-free while policy bank financial bonds are not), changes in the positioning of policy banks, the relative credit of local governments and so on. To simplify the discussion, Treasury is considered as the representative of government bonds in this article. Regarding bonds of different terms, the one-year Treasury bonds represent short-term government bonds and the 10-year ones represent the long-term ones. The following is about the transmission from money market rate to short-term government bonds.

China's academic community and market has basically yielded no fruit on the transmission logic from money market to short-term government bonds. However, the experience from the US, the European Union, Singapore, Canada, South Korea, India, Thailand, Mexico and others shows that there exists a significant correlation between money market rate and short-term Treasury interest rates. In the following analysis, overnight rate is considered as the money market rate and the one-year Treasury interest rate as short-term interest rate. The data of their monthly average is smoothed and shown in Figure 6.6, followed by statistical analysis. The focus is on two issues: (1) Is overnight rate related to one-year Treasury yield? (2) What is the average spread between overnight rate and one-year Treasury?

In the case of the US, its one-year Treasury is highly correlated with federal fund rate, showing almost no deviation, as shown in Figure 6.6. The linear regression of the data from 1954 to 2014 shows that their R^2 is as high as 0.96. As the federal fund rate in the US is completely determined by the federal fund rate target set by the Fed, the one-year Treasury can be seen as determined by the Fed's federal fund rate target. The mean value of spread between the one-year Treasury and federal fund rate is 7BP (arrived at through calculating the average of one-year Treasury monthly yield mean value minus federal fund rate monthly mean value), and the median of that is 16BP.

In the case of Thailand, the monthly average of overnight rate and that of one-year Treasury yield from 2005 to 2014 also shows obvious correlation. R^2 of their linear regression is 0.92, indicating very high correlation. The mean value of spread between one-year Treasury and overnight rate monthly average is 19BP and the median is 21BP.

Figure 6.6 US one-year Treasury yield moves in the direction consistent with federal fund rate. (Citation: WIND)

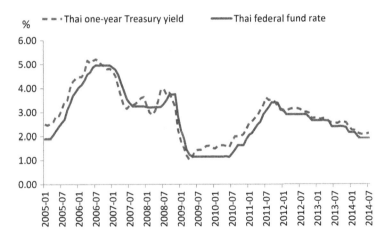

Figure 6.7 Thai one-year Treasury yield moves in the direction consistent with federal fund rate. (Citation: WIND)

Table 6.1 shows the spread and relevant analysis of the US, the European Union, Singapore, Canada, South Korea, India, Thailand, Mexico and so on. The correlation coefficient between overnight rate and one-year Treasury yield in all these countries is basically above 0.9 and the average stands at 0.94. The one-year Treasury yield in all these countries is higher than overnight rate, which is mainly attributable to the positive maturity

Table 6.1   Correlation between one-year Treasury yield and overnight rate in major countries

	Correlation coefficient (R^2)	Average	Median
USA	0.96	7	16
European Union	0.97	5	4
Singapore	0.98	19	23
Canada	0.95	15	11
South Korea	0.87	42	35
India	0.91	45	28
Thailand	0.92	19	21
Mexico	0.94	26	16
mean value	0.94	22	19

premium. The spread between the two in each country is different, being relatively smaller in developed economies with advanced markets such as the US and the European Union and 20–40BP in other countries. Such differences may be related to the differences in the liquidity of one-year Treasury in these countries. In developed countries with advanced bond market, one-year Treasury can be easily cashed in; thus its disadvantage of longer term is offset by the advantage of greater liquidity. From the perspective of term structure theory, the less segmented the long-term (one-year) and the short-term (overnight) are from each other in the market, the more correlated the interest rates of the two and the less the added term premium will be. This chapter basically conforms to this expectation.

In conclusion, international experience reveals that one-year Treasury yield and overnight rate are highly correlated based on two major reasons: first, the high-level liquidity of one-year Treasury determines that the Treasury yield directly hinges on liquidity rather than the fundamentals; second, the strong cashability and high-level liquidity of one-year Treasury makes it a good substitute for overnight interbank lending. The average of one-year Treasury minus overnight rate, which stands at around 5–45BP in major countries, is related to how advanced the bond market in a country is. In summary, the mean value of spread between one-year Treasury and overnight rate is around 20BP. The following research focuses on the relationship between China's money market and bond market.

Transmission from Money Market to Short-Term Government Bonds in the Chinese Market

The transmission relationship from the money market to the bond market in China is not clear; thus, it is controversial to match one-year Treasury yield with overnight market. Historically, the monthly average of overnight rate has been volatile even though the statistics at some time points (for example, June of 2013 and the Spring Festival of each year) are excluded; one-year Treasury and overnight rate have not been moving in a consistent direction like in other countries. Statistically, the correlation coefficient R^2 between the two was only 0.63 from 2003 and 2014, much lower than the international level.

If we consider China's money market rate as a piecewise function, the correlation between one-year Treasury and money market rate will be increased significantly. It can be seen from Figure 6.8 that systemic changes happened to the correlation between overnight rate and one-year Treasury after the financial crisis of 2008. Before 2008, one-year Treasury yield was obviously higher than overnight rate and overnight rate seemed to play a leading role. After 2008, although overnight rate is more volatile than one-year Treasury yield, their movement is significantly correlated and highly synchronized. The correlation coefficient R^2 between the two from 2009 to 2014 reached 0.83, basically comparable to that of international level.

Figure 6.8   Comparison of one-year Treasury and overnight rate in China. (Citation: WIND)

In terms of the spread between one-year Treasury and overnight rate, its mean value stands at 24BP and the median 27BP from 2009 and 2014, which are above average compared with those of other countries. The spread in China is lower than that of South Korea and India but higher than most other countries, close to the spread average of 20BP.

Regarding China's bond market, two issues are worth our attention:

(a) Why was the relationship between one-year Treasury and money market rate so different before and after 2008?

I think the answer lies in the Treasury market and money market being unsound. Specifically speaking: (1) the transaction volume of the Treasury market is quite small. The transaction volume of Treasury bonds was only 2.6 trillion RMB in 2004, but stood at 63.6 trillion RMB in 2010, which was 24 times that of 2004. Before 2008, due to inadequate liquidity of treasury, its liquidity premium did not emerge, thus the spread between it and interbank lending interest rate was quite huge. (2) Among the market factors responsible for Treasury pricing, information on fundamentals accounted for a too large share and liquidity accounted for a share smaller than that after 2008. One piece of evidence is that R^2 between one-year Treasury and ten-year Treasury before 2008 was 0.7 and this figure dropped to 0.6 after 2008. (3) SHIBOR as the basic interest rate system was formally rolled out in 2007 and it provided stronger guidance for the pricing of short-term products. At the same time, transaction volume of pledge-style repurchase increased significantly to RMB 15.7 trillion in 2005 and to RMB 84.7 trillion in 2010. The standing of money market in the financial system became significantly higher.

(b) Since 2014, the average spread between one-year Treasury and overnight rate has been 70BP, obviously higher than it historically was in China and also high internationally. What is the reason for that?

• The money market rate is not effective. Although China's money market rate is determined by banks independently, daily transactions reveal that the transaction price of the day basically hovers around the opening price but is tainted by the will of the central bank and the interests of major banks. Because of this, market participants often feel that lending is not available although transaction interest rate is quite low. This means that the money market rate in China is not effective as it should be. A further explanation is as follows: the central bank of China does not consider money market rate as a target of its operation, thus it will not issue money to maintain a certain rate, in other words, the central bank does not participate in the money market operation except the open market operations on every Tuesday and Thursday. In other countries, overnight rate is usually considered as the benchmark rate and the central banks directly participate in market transactions. These central banks also have indefinite resources to maintain market interest rate at a satisfactory level. China's opening price partially serves as the benchmark, but market participants do not have enough resources to maintain the benchmark.

• The expectation is uncertain. The logic behind the transmission from the money market to one-year Treasury is that the market can obtain capital through the stable rollover of overnight rate and the average interest rate during a year of rollover is overnight rate itself, which is the yield of one-year Treasury. In other words, the term premium between one-year Treasury and overnight is 0, because the central banks promise no change to the interest rate for a long period of time under price-based regulation. In China, the absence of similar promises leads to huge uncertainty with the overnight rate expectation next year in the market, which results in an increase in the term premium between one-year Treasury and overnight rate. These two factors determine that China's spread between one-year Treasury yield and overnight rate when the quantity-based regulation is the main form is higher than the average in major countries. In conclusion, China's one-year Treasury and overnight rate still obviously correlate overall, especially after 2009 when the transaction of Treasury and inter-banking lending increased significantly and after the SHIBOR pricing mechanism was rolled out. Considering that the shift of China's money policies away from quantity-based regulation to price-based regulation is certain, we can learn from international experience that the money market rate will be gradually less volatile, which will be more of a guidance for the pricing of one-year Treasury. In the longer run, with the deepening of the Treasury market, the spread between one-year Treasury and overnight rate will continue to decrease. As the average of money market interest rate gradually stabilizes, the gap between the expectation and the reality of liquidity will narrow down and the spread between one-year Treasury and overnight rate will arrive at global average of 20–30BP.

Deconstruction of the Spread Between One-Year Treasury and Overnight Rate

I believe that one-year Treasury yield – overnight rate = term spread – credit spread – liquidity premium, in which term spread refers to the term spread between one-year Treasury and overnight lending (please note that this is different from the term spread between 10-year Treasury and one-year Treasury in the next section), credit spread refers to the credit spread between Treasury and super triple – A corporate bonds (as the interbank lending counterpart is ordinary banks rather than central banks), and liquidity premium means that Treasury can be cashed in advance while interbank lending cannot.

The components of the above formula, the various kinds of spread, can be deconstructed to further analyze the factors that influence the spread and explain the obvious amplification of the spread between the one-year Treasury and overnight rate in 2014.

One-year Treasury yield – overnight rate
= (one-year treasury – one-year super triple – A corporate bonds) + (one-year super triple – A corporate bonds – one-year interbank lending interest rate) + (one-year interbank lending interest rate – overnight rate)
= (one-year interbank lending interest rate – overnight rate) – (one-year super triple – A corporate bonds-one-year treasury) – (one-year interbank lending interest rate – one-year super triple – A corporate bonds).

In this formula, the three constituents on the right side of the equal sign are approximately seen as term spread, credit spread, and liquidity premium respectively. The data processing results are as shown in Table 6.2. It is worth noting that the difference between the positive sign and the negative sign means that the spread between one-year Treasury and overnight rate increases if term spread increases and the overall spread decreases if credit spread and liquidity premium increase.

Table 6.2 Deconstruction of China's spread between one-year Treasury and overnight rate

	Average (2010–2014)%	Average (from 201.1) (%)	**Margin (BP)**
Term spread	2.11	2.70	59
Credit spread	1.36	1.56	19
Liquidity premium	0.53	0.43	–10
Spread between one-year Treasury and overnight rate	0.22	0.71	49

In short, the huge increase of term spread by 59BP is the main reason for the expansion of the spread between one-year Treasury and overnight rate. In addition, the increase of the spread between corporate bonds and Treasury by 19BP partially hedged against the influence of higher term spread. Liquidity premium was decreased by a small margin by 10BP, making an overall positive contribution to the spread.

The analysis result above conforms to the theoretical analysis in the last section that the spread between one-year Treasury and overnight rate expands mainly because there exists a significant difference between the capital interest rate in reality and the expected one, which is reflected in the huge expansion of term spread. Thus, if the central bank can adopt measures to maintain the stability of the money market rate, the gap between the expectation for future funds and the interest rate in reality will be smaller, and a smaller term spread will lead the spread between one-year Treasury and overnight rate to fall back to historical average.

Transmission from the Short-Term to the Long-Term Government Bonds

The traditional definition of term spread is the difference between the long-term and short-term government bonds. Generally, term spread reflects the expectations for future economic fundamentals. In the last section, term spread referred to the difference between one-year and overnight rates and reflects the expectations for the liquidity of the central bank over a period of time. It is different from the traditional term spread. This section will focus on how short-term interest rate is transmitted to the long-term rates of government bonds, namely the decisive factors for the term spread between 10-year and one-year rates.

There are three major theories for term spread: first, the expectation theory that regards long-term interest rate as short-term rate expectation; second, market segmentation theory that holds short-term bonds and long-term bonds as two independent markets priced by supply and demand; and third, liquidity preference theory that regards long-term bonds and short-term bonds as mutually related except that liquidity premium is required for long-term bonds as the liquidity of long-term bonds is lower. I think all three theories are plausible, but they can only explain bond markets of different development phases. The expectation theory suits the bond markets of developed countries in Europe and the United States while China is best explained by liquidity preference theory. This section will first discuss the decisive factors of term spread theories, conduct case studies of European and American bond markets and finally make an analysis of bond market in China.

According to the expectation theory, spot interest rate of long-term bonds is the average of short-term rate expectation over a period of time in future. Therefore, we should analyze the effect of incident shock on expectation for future rates. Generally, rate expectation in a relatively short time is dependent on the continuation of the central bank's monetary policies while long-term rate expectation depends on the changes of economic fundamentals. We will discuss the expectation theory in two scenarios and prove my argument with the case study of European and American bond markets.

First, if the central bank does not change short-term rates, the long-term interest rates depend only on the changes of expectation for future. Therefore, if the economy prospers or the inflation rate increases, expectation for future rate rise will increase and the average of different terms of expected rate will be higher than the real interest rate, leading to a rise in term spread. Therefore, if the short-term rate remains the same, the long-term rate will depend on the increase or decrease of rate expectation by the central bank because of changes in economic fundamentals. As shown in Figure 6.9, the euro zone has remained the same short-term rate since 2012 and the core Consumer Price Index (CPI) has been decreasing gradually. Therefore, the yield of 10-year government bonds has been decreasing as well.

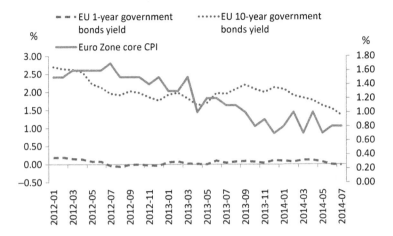

Figure 6.9 Term spread is related to economic fundamentals. (Citation: WIND)

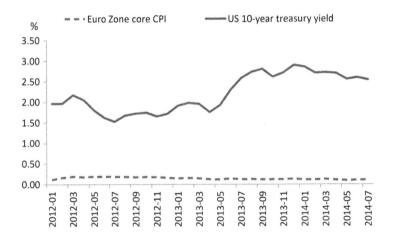

Figure 6.10 Expectation for QE exit causes a rise in long-term rate. (Citation: WIND)

In addition to economic fundamentals, the long-term rate also depends on the expectation management of the central bank, namely the direct intervention of the central bank on future rate expectation when the short-term rate remains the same. As shown in Figure 6.10, the Federal Reserve released the signal of ending Quantitative Easing (QE) and increasing interest rate in the first half of 2013, leading to strong expectations from the market and a rapid adjustment of the yield of 10-year government bond in the second quarter of 2013. It is worth noticing that the Federal Reserve did not put a real end to QE until December 2013. As the market already adjusted expectations of ending QE, the actual move of the Federal Reserve did not cause a big rise in the yield of government bonds. There was even a decrease in the yield of 10-year government bonds. Therefore, the expectations of long-term bond are more effective than actual market operations.

Second, when the central bank raises interest rate in an overheating economy and high inflation, it will directly cause a rise in short-term rate. There are expectations for increasing rate by the central bank over a period of time in future and therefore the expected rate for future will surpass real interest rate. As time goes on, the market has lower expectations of economic growth and inflation caused by a higher interest rate. If the central bank adopts Taylor's rule or similar monetary policy rules, there will be expectations of lowering the rate by the central bank over a long time in future and interest rate expectation will be lower than real rate. As time goes on, expectations of future economic fundamentals are more important and the average of various terms of interest rate will be reduced. To put it briefly, expectations of lower long-term rate mainly depend on expectations of future fundamentals and decreasing inflation. If the short-term rate rises, the term spread will be reduced. If the short-term rate goes down, expectations of economic growth, higher inflation and the central bank's rate raise will cause bigger term spread. In 2004, the increased long-term rate is smaller than the short-term rate after the rate raise of the Federal Reserve, leading to narrowed term spread. In 2007, the term spread becomes bigger because the decreased long-term rate is smaller than short-term rate after the rate cut of the Fed.

In conclusion, when the short-term rate remains the same, term spread depends on the changes in economic fundamentals and the effect of the central bank's expectation management. When the short-term rate increases, the long-term rate increases, only at slower pace, and therefore term spread is narrowed. When the short-term rate drops, the long-term rate decreases at slower pace as well, causing bigger term spread. In

Figure 6.11   Relationship of term spread and rate change. (Citation: WIND)

addition, as 40% of American government bonds are held by foreign investors who prefer long-term investment, there has been market segmentation of long-term and short-term rate. Therefore, global capital flow affects term spread as well. The section will not elaborate on that in detail.

Let us turn to the decisive factors of term spread in China's government bonds. The government bonds market in China is relatively backward and it suits the liquidity preference theory better than the expectation theory in the early development stage. According to the expectation theory, when the short-term rate goes up, the long-term rate increases as well, only at slower pace, and the term spread becomes smaller. However, in China's bond market from 2003 to 2005, the increased long-term rate is much higher than short-term rate, respectively 2% and less than 1%. The possible reasons are less liquidity of long-term government bonds in bear market and higher liquidity premium required. Market expectation is another major cause. The market has strong expectations of bear market and irrational factors such as market sentiment have led to the big difference between the real development of bond market and theoretical expectation.

The expectation theory suits the next two cycles, which indicates the maturing of Chinese bond market. Let us take the rate increase in 2010 in Figure 6.13 as an example. When the short-term rate soars, the long-term

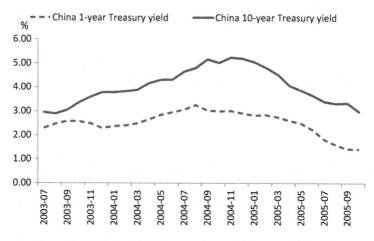

Figure 6.12 "Irrational" bear market in 2004. (Citation: WIND)

Figure 6.13 Expectation theory in Chinese bond market. (Citation: WIND)

rate increases at a slower pace and remains the same after reaching a certain level. It is no more affected by the rise of short-term rate. This indicates the fact that the long-term high growth and inflation in high-interest rate have been weakened greatly and there are expectations of the decrease of long-term rate.

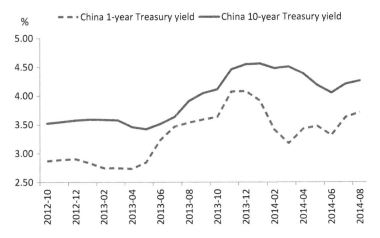

Figure 6.14   Another failure of the expectation theory. (Citation: WIND)

However, the market in the second half of 2013 is different. As shown in Figure 6.14, there is a mismatch between long-term interest rate and short-term rate. The one-year government bond increases and decreases prior to the change of 10-year government bond from May 2013 to June 2014. This is unprecedented in Chinese bond market and it cannot be explained by the expectation theory. When one-year Government bond starts increasing, 10-year bond remains the same and the term spread becomes smaller. This is in accordance with the expectation theory. However, in early 2014, the short-term rate stops increasing while the long-term rate continues to go up, leading to bigger term spread. According to the expectation theory, there will be expectations of economic growth and inflation in market. But in reality, the market was very pessimistic about Chinese economy. In the first quarter of 2014, the short-term rate dropped greatly while the long-term rate remained the same, which could have been a signal of optimistic expectations for the economy. But indicators such as industrial added value continued to plunge and the market expectations were even more pessimistic. More interestingly, during the second quarter of 2014, the long-term rate plunged and the term spread narrowed greatly, which could have indicated pessimistic expectations for growth and inflation according to the expectation theory.

But in fact, industrial added value and PMI gradually recovered and the market had positive expectations for Chinese economy. I think that this is caused by the time lapse between 10-year and one-year bond yield and term spread was not an effective indicator for this period.

I think the reason behind this rare phenomenon is that the factors affecting bond market have changed. Before 2013, Chinese bond market basically matched China's fundamentals, especially in terms of its response to inflation cycle. In other words, the bond market abides by the traditional Taylor's rule. In the second half of 2013, however, China's interest rate climbed up due to liquidity instead of fundamentals. The yield rate decline in 2014 was also attributed to the liquidity factor. So liquidity perfectly explains the performance of the bond market: the liquidity-driven bond-yield changes have become irrelevant with fundamentals and they are directly determined by the money market and the liquidity management of the People's Bank of China; so fundamentals are no longer effective in anticipating long-term interest rates, which leads to difficulties in anticipating long-term rates. This has led to the fact that expected rate is slow in its response to the real rate: i.e., continuing high-rising real rate will change theoretical expectation of interest rate and push long-term government bond's yield rate; continuing sluggish real rate will change long-term expectation as well and lower long-term government bond's yield rate. It takes long observation to anticipate future interest rate based on the current real rate, which means long-term expectation is possible only when the trend of short-term interest rate has become clear. The time required for observation is the lag between short-term and long-term interest rates. Although the expectation theory for long-term government bond's yield rate still applies, the bond market is behaving differently because the traditional Taylor's rule no longer applies to interest expectation.

In conclusion, the expectation theory is suitable for foreign bond markets and there is no single explanation for bond market in China because of the immaturity of Chinese financial market. For the primary phase of bond market, liquidity preference theory is more plausible, namely strong market segmentation and weak bond liquidity. From 2005 to 2013, the expectation theory suits the bond market in China but more adjustment should be made to the expectation theory to explain the bond market from 2013 to 2014.

SECTION THREE: "MONEY MARKET → CREDIT MARKET" TRANSMISSION MECHANISM

The transmission from the money market to the credit market is a rarely discussed topic in China. There are mainly two reasons. First, China's interest rate control means that lending and deposit rates are independent of the monetary market. In other words, lending and deposit rates are determined by the central bank, while the money market interest rate is subject to the market where the central bank seldom directly intervenes. Second, although the control on lending rates was lifted in 2013, lending rates have little to do with the money market, because in China, lending rates are calculated based on the comprehensive financing cost of banks whose liabilities are mainly deposits. As a result, since 2014, some in the market have begun to hold that the central bank's efforts to maintain low money-market interest rates are useless in reducing the financing cost in real economy that mainly relies on loans to get financed. But international experiences have shown that in a country where interest rates are liberalized, deposit and lending rates highly correlate with the central bank's benchmark interest rates (which are almost the same with interest rates on money market or quasi money market). It is indicated that there exists a transmission from the money market to the credit market. At the same time, China's experiences show that there is a time lag between the two markets. I believe that although deposit rates are controlled in China, there are several transmission channels from the money market to the credit market.

This section reviews the relationship between lending rates and money-market interest rates in China's early years and then discusses the transmission mechanism from the money market to lending rates.

Benchmark Interest Rates' Impact on Lending and Deposit Rates — International Experiences

Money-market interest rates, when taken as the benchmark, greatly impact lending and deposit rates. But we cannot hold that the interest rates, once liberalized, are totally determined by players in the market other than the central bank. In contrast, the central bank has an indirect but major influence on interest rates in the deposit and loan markets.

First, we consider the money-market interest rates' impacts on the deposit rate. The impacts are direct and huge, because money market loans can be replaced with deposits. If there is a huge difference between the two rates, the deposit rate will be definitely approaching the money-market interest rate. That is because money-market interest rates that are directly controlled by the central bank are steady, but the deposit rate, by comparison, is more flexible. Suppose the interest rate in the money market is 1% and deposit rate, 3%. Then banks may seek financing in the money market, which will reduce the demand for deposits. Since money-market interest rate is lower, people may reduce investment in monetary funds and increase deposits, thus raising the supply of deposits. As the demand goes down and the supply up, the deposit rate will decline to the level of money-market interest rate. It can also be understood as covered interest arbitrage between the money market and the deposit market. With a lot of arbitrage going on, potential profit is declining. As a result, the deposit rate is dropping close to the federal target interest rate. Take South Korea as an example. Since 2002, the spread between the 3-month term deposit rate and the benchmark rate has been around 0.1–0.6%. This strongly showcases how the substitution relationship between money-market loans and deposits can level the difference between the deposit rate and the benchmark rate.

Money-market interest rates also greatly impact the lending rate. In the US, for example, the prime rate (at which companies with good credit can get loans, similar to China's LPR) is 3% plus the US benchmark rate, or the federal funds rate (which can be seen as the overnight money market rate). The other lending rates are calculated as the prime rate plus credit spreads. Of course, 3% is not prescribed by the central bank, but agreed upon by commercial banks and companies. In fact, since 1992, except in 2008 when the extreme situation happened, the spread has fluctuated from 2.95% to 3.20%, which can be approximately deemed as a fixed value. As a result, the transmission from the money market to the loan market goes like this: the central bank → the benchmark rate in the money market → the benchmark rate in the credit market → the lending rate.

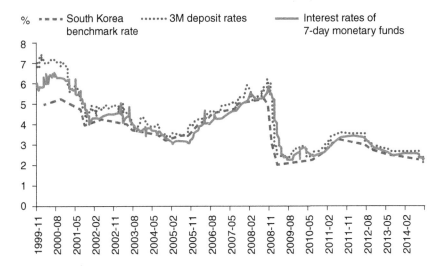

Figure 6.15 In South Korea, deposit rates and interest rates of monetary funds are almost solely determined by the benchmark rate. (Citation: WIND)

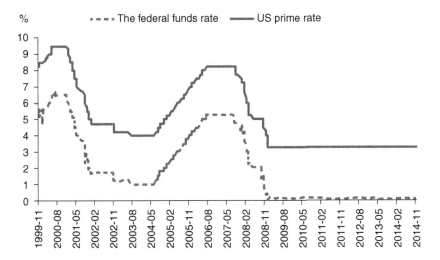

Figure 6.16 In the US, the prime rate is almost solely determined by the federal funds rate. (Citation: WIND)

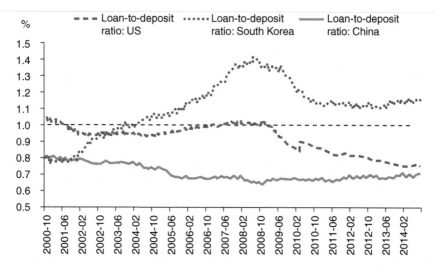

Figure 6.17   In the US and South Korea where interest rates are liberalized, the loan-to-deposit ratio is much higher than China's, even exceeding 100%.

(*Note*: Most countries do not have official calculations for the loan-to-deposit ratio. In Figure 6.17 the "loans" and "deposits" mean all commercial banks' loans and leases, and all commercial banks' deposits for the US; loans of both commercial banks and specialized banks, and deposits of both commercial banks and specialized banks for South Korea; outstanding loans of financial institutions, and outstanding deposits for China. (Citation: WIND)

It should be pointed out here that the connectivity between the interbank market and the credit market is the basis of the transmission from the central bank's benchmark rate to other interest rates. In China, these two markets are segmented. The main reason is that deposits and interbank lending play very different roles for China's banks. The requirement of loan-to-deposit ratio means loans are possible only when there are deposits. In the US and South Korea where interest rates are liberalized, total loans outstrip total deposits, which means there are loans through interbank liabilities. In China, however, although there are no specified bans, banks have no practical need for such loans, because the requirement of loan-to-deposit ratio necessarily leads to the oversupply of deposits. But if the requirement of loan-to-deposit ratio is removed, maturity mismatch in the money market will lead to a spike of interest rates and systematic financial risks. Here, I want to mention the "No.127 Document" which regulates the ratio of interbank liabilities to overall liabilities. Such regulations are not appropriate if interest rates are liberalized, but as China is going through a transition, they are quite reasonable.

Relationship Between the Money Market and the Deposit and Loan Markets in China

Now have a look at China. Figure 6.18 is about the money-market interest rate and the lending rate. Their change trends show a basically positive correlation. But this does not seem to be enough to justify the transmission from the money market to the credit market, because one explanation for their correlation before 2012 can be that the two rates were both subject to the central bank's monetary policies (for example, lowering reserve requirement, and interest rates). In the second half of 2013, in particular, as the money-market interest rate soared, the lending rate remained steady. This is a major reason why the market believes money-market interest rates have little to do with lending rates.

In addition, the change of lending rates lags behind that of money-market interest rates for two possible reasons. One is statistical reason. Weighted lending rates are published quarterly, but money-market interest rates are published monthly. There is a time lag. If we match the lending rates

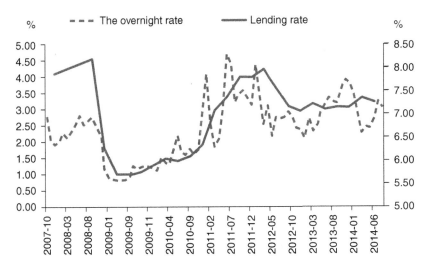

Figure 6.18   The overnight rate is in positive correlation with the lending rate. (Citation: WIND)

with the beginning of a quarter, the time lag in 2011–2012 will disappear. The other reason is the steadiness of the lending rate. As loans are negotiated by banks and customers, and not totally determined by the market, the influence of the central bank's monetary policies will be felt later in loans.

As is mentioned at the beginning of this section, loans, compared with the bond market, are quite independent of the money market. As a result, it is reasonable that the market separates the credit market from the money market. But I think there is transmission from the money market to the credit market. I will explain why from theoretical and empirical perspectives.

A major difference between China and the US is that in China, the deposit rate is not liberalized. It is the root reason why the credit market is separated from the money market. But we should also see that with the liberalization of interest rates, the quasi-deposit financial products that are not subject to regulations on interest rates are developing fast. Since banks' liabilities are partly under the influence of the market and assets completely subject to the market, a transmission channel as in the US also exists in China.

If banks' liabilities are completely subject to the market, the lending rate is mainly determined by banks' financing cost. That is,

Lending rate = Banks' financing cost + Relatively fixed spread.

The pricing of loans is quite different from that of bonds. Bond yields are related with the risk-free rate, but lending rates depends on banks' financing cost. In some countries, the financing cost is also closely related to the risk-free rate. But it is not the situation in China because of the tight control on deposit rates.

In general, the spread of China's commercial banks is 2–3%. It can be taken as an independent variable because it is related to how liberalized the market is and the relative premium probability of depositors, banks, and corporations, instead of risk-free interest rate. Therefore, the key to the channel from the money market to the credit market is how the money market impacts the cost of bank financing. The equation of banks' financing costs is:

Banks' financing costs = Rigid costs + Non-rigid costs.

In the above equation, rigid costs are deposit costs, directly regulated by central bank's deposit interest rate. Non-rigid costs include highly liberalized costs such as interbank borrowing costs, financing costs, and bond issue costs. In banks, all the capital first flows into allocation department and then allocated to various assets. Therefore, loan interest rate does not solely relate to deposit interest rate, but is a comprehensive cost incorporating non-rigid costs. Loan interest rate greatly resembles financing cost. At the beginning of 2014, the yield of financial products reached a record high, the loan interest rate then increased. Compared to money market, the yield of financial products fluctuates moderately and influences the banks' costs directly. The connection between financing and loan interest rate indicates that non-rigid costs do influence loan interest rates.

I believe the money market mainly influences the credit market through non-rigid cost. Also, financial products and deposits can substitute one another; deposits of residents and corporations can be converted into financial products and deposit savings. Consequently, when the interest rate of financial products changes, the proportion of non-rigid and rigid costs will change. In addition, corporations can choose their ways of financing in forms of bonds, notes, or loans, hence the three ways are convergent.

Specifically, money market influences the credit market in the following aspects: (1) the interest rate of money market influences interbank borrowing costs; (2) the interest rate of money market influences wealth management costs; (3) the interest rate of money market influences banks'

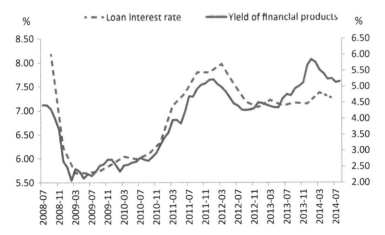

Figure 6.19   Loan interest rate positively relates to yield of financial products. (Citation: WIND)

bond issue cost; (4) the interest rate of money market influences the scale and proportion of financial products and deposit savings; (5) the commercial paper market and the bond market, influenced by the money market, can substitute the credit market. Compared to the US, China lacks only one aspect of influence: the interest rate of money market influences deposit costs. However, China's wealth management products have taken up part of the channel from the money market interest to the deposit interest rate. I will discuss the above six channels and display data to see if China's money market influences loan interest rate.

First, the interest rate of money market influences interbank borrowing costs. Interbank borrowing is one of banks' major non-rigid costs. As is shown in Figure 6.20, stock-holding banks' interbank debt to total liability is kept at 10–30%, with some exceeding 25%. If the interest rate of money market is lowered, the cost of interbank borrowing will decrease, hence banks' comprehensive cost is lowered, and to some extent, leads to lower loan interest rate.

Second, interest rate of money market influences wealth management costs. Before 2013, there was no way to determine the relation between

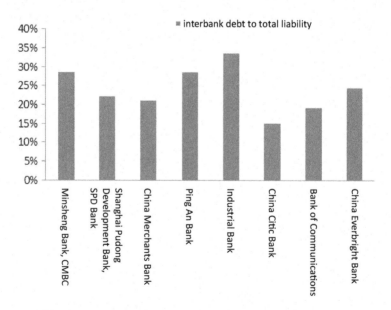

Figure 6.20 Commercial banks' interbank debt to total liability.

the two, because they both respond to central bank's increase or decrease of interest rate. After 2013, we can confirm that as the interest rate of money market increases, the yield of financial products also goes up, and vice versa. Worth noticing is that compared to the interest rate of money market, the interest rate of financial products lag behind by 1 to 3 months, indicating higher stickiness. The money market influences the interest rate of financial products because money market and financial products are non-rigid costs for banks and both are apparently substitutive. If the interest rate of money market is relatively low, the demand for financial funds is weak, which leads to lower interest rate of financial products. This conduction mechanism is identical with the US money market interest rate and deposit interest rate.

In China, the lag of interest rate of financial products and money market is due to the following three factors: (1) Compared with the United States, the interest rate of money market fluctuates significantly. The data accumulated in a short term does not indicate the trend; hence the interest rate of financial products cannot be adjusted with proper aims before the trend is predicted. (2) Compared with the United States, the Federal Reserve directly declares the target interest rate of money market; hence the interest rate of the entire market is adjusted toward the goal in a quick manner. But in China, the target interest rate of money market is not set, so the trend of interest rate is hard to predict. (3) The financial products are more customer-sticky. Banks face the difficulty in adjusting the interest rate of financial products in large scale in the short run. Loans are sticky for a similar reason. For your information, according to China's current banking system, deposits are the scarcest resource because the deposits, financial products, and financing in the money market cannot be fully substituted, and because of the limitation of the loan-to-deposit ratio and the scale of interbank borrowing. After the loan-to-deposit ratio is liberalized, it will be easier to influence interest rate of money market and loans through financing.

Third, interest rate of money market influences banks' bond issue cost. This channel is mainly targeted at bank's financing through issuing bonds. Up until June 2014, total deposit reached 110 trillion RMB, of which banks' financing through issuing bonds accounts for 11 trillion RMB, taking up 10% total deposit. This ratio maintained the same since

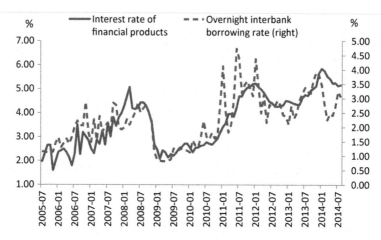

Figure 6.21 Overnight interbank borrowing rate positively relates to interest rate of financial products. (Citation: WIND)

2012, but it may increase. According to the documents for adjusting the deposit-to-loan ratio released by the CBRC on June 30, 2014, financing used for supporting agriculture and SMEs should not be accounted into the deposit-to-loan ratio. This document provided legal channels to facilitate the banks to breakthrough deposit to loan ratio. Banks have the incentive to issue more financial bonds. The financing costs of financial bonds are closely related to money market interest rate. Therefore, the money market interest rate can influence the banks' financing cost in issuing bonds, and may further influence the loan interest rate. In addition, the liabilities of China's policy banks are mainly bonds, while the assets are loans. Policy banks work as the bridge between bonds and loans. The future banks may be further "state-dominated." The combination of bonds and loans will facilitate the money market interest rate to be the channels for credit market through bonds.

Fourth, interest rate of money market influences the scale and proportion of financial products and deposit savings. Even though the money market interest rate cannot directly influence deposit interest rate, people can choose freely between depositing their money and investing in financial products. Therefore, the two choices are substitutive. If the interest rate of financial products goes up, people prefer to buy financial products,

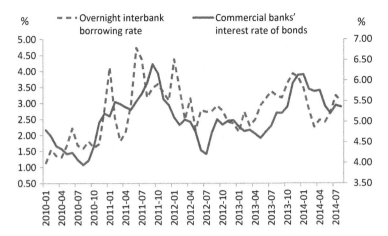

Figure 6.22 Overnight interbank borrowing rate positively relates to commercial banks' interest rate of bonds. (Citation: WIND)

hence less deposit, and vice versa. On the other hand, if banks can finance from money market with relatively low interest rate, corporations will have much less "deposit" through financing. If money squeeze occurs in money market, banks have to attract deposit through high interest rate of wealth management products. Figure 6.23 shows that compared to the same period, deposit has a periodic negative relation with the yields of wealth management products. This is not solely the result of the substitution effect mentioned in this paragraph. Specifically, before 2012, the interest rate of financial products resembles the base rate of deposits. This periodic trend indicates that after the central bank lowered the interest rate and adopted loose monetary policy, the National Development and Reform Commission (NDRC) will approve a large sum of loans for different projects, which will lead to the climb of deposit increase rate. On the contrary, the increase in interest rate means the central bank adopts tight monetary policy and deposits will grow slower. After July 2012, the interest rate of savings maintained the same. The interest rate of deposits and financial products are unpegged. Only when the yield of financial products negatively relates to the increase in deposit in the same period, will it support this theory to some extent. Relatively speaking, the higher the interest rate of financial products, the faster the growth of financial

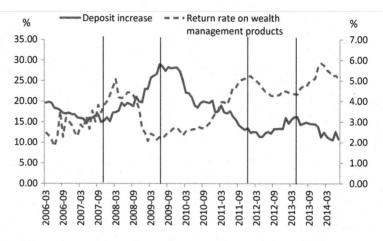

Figure 6.23   Negative correlation between deposit increase and the return rate on wealth management products. (Citation: WIND)

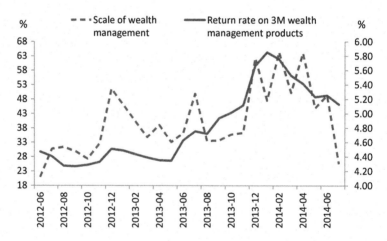

Figure 6.24   Positive correlation between the scale of wealth management and its return rate. (Citation: WIND)

products. In addition, the current scale of financial products is about 15 trillion RMB, and that of deposit 110 trillion RMB. The scale differs apparently and it cannot fully support the substitution effect. It is safe to estimate that as the scale of financial products increases, the substitution effect will be enhanced. The interest rate of money market will also exert greater influence on the banks through financial products.

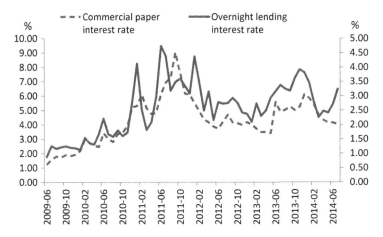

Figure 6.25   Positive correlation between commercial paper interest rate and overnight lending interest rate.

Fifth, the commercial paper market under the influence of the money market is an alternative to the bond market and the credit market. The commercial paper market is where corporations seek short-term financing. Given business services like purchase of commercial papers under agreements to resell and that the maturities of bills are more similar to the money market than loans, commercial paper interest rates are more close to those in the money market than of loans. Since the second quarter of 2014, interest rates in the commercial paper market have been dropping, a deviation from the money market. This is largely because bank loans to corporations are confined to less than one year, as banks are unwilling to offer money. In some way, commercial papers, bonds and credit loans are alternatives of corporate financing. Since commercial paper interest rates are highly related to bond interest rates and money market interest rates, when the interest rate in the money market declines, companies prefer financing through commercial papers and bonds to credit loans. With fewer restrictions on bond issuance and more direct financing, such a preference will be more prominent.

In conclusion, despite the currently weak direct relation between money market interest rate and loan interest rate, multiple channels are still available from the money market interest rate to the loan interest rate. This is largely because part of the deposit market and the loan market are highly marketized, making most financial products and financing methods replaceable. According to international experience, when interest rate is fully liberalized, the loan interest will be fully marketized, bringing the money market interest rate and the loan interest rate together. Once the central bank decides on price-based adjustment and chooses money market interest rate as the benchmark interest rate, the channel from the money market to the deposit and lending interest rates will be much wider.

SECTION FOUR: ANALYSIS FRAMEWORK FOR THE BOND MARKET — "THE REVISED TAYLOR'S RULE"

In the third section, we have talked about the channels from the benchmark interest rate to the short-term government bonds and from the short-term government bonds to the long-term government bonds. But such analysis is not relevant to China's bond market. This is because in China's money market and bond market, the money market interest rate is subject to big swings, as it is not the "benchmark" but determined independently by the market activities, including banks' short-term activities and demand for large deposits in particular times. In the long run, the interest rate in our money market is decided by inflation, different from the return rate on long-term government bonds. In general, it is hard to predict the interest rate in the money market as much as the interest rate in the bond market. Moreover, the determinants of term spread are complex, making it unfeasible to predict the return rate on long-term bonds through "money market interest rate + term spread."

This section will provide an analysis framework for the bond market based on the "Revised Taylor's Rule." I believe the return rate on long-term government bonds is governed by the "Revised Taylor's Rule." The three primary factors are growth gap, inflation gap and financial system risks while in special times, supply and demand, politics and public sentiment should also be factored in. The spread on long-term credit loans are determined by "corporate default risk premium + bond liquidity premium," the latter of which usually gets the upper hand.

In the beginning of this section, I need to put forward a basic premise: the so-called "bond supply and demand" has never been the determinant in China's bond market. Some hold that the supply of government bonds is determined by financial deficit whereas the demand depends on the scale of government bonds allocation by the three groups of allocating institutions — banks, insurance companies and funds. By comparing the two figures, we can know the supply and demand to predict the trend of government bond yield. In such a perspective, bonds are considered as a common commodity that has both producers and consumers. Consumers' demand for the bonds is decided by the inelastic demand for allocated government bonds. However, I must point out that bonds are more of a financial good with investment values than a common good. For any financial good, the demand is determined by "the deviation of the price from the value." For example, when the allocating institutions allocate × billion government bonds, if the price of government bonds is lower than the value, there will be an opportunity for profit or even arbitrage, which will boost the demand for those bonds. This pushes "trading organiza- tions" to continue trading bonds even when the price has deviated from the value until the two figures come close. By and large, allocating institu- tions hold bond positions way larger than trading organizations, but with far less flexibility. Moreover, trading organizations are the marginal factor that affects the supply and demand of bonds; the bond price is determined by the marginal price rather than the allocating price that involves no transaction. This section will explain in length that the so-called "supply and demand factors" can only play a key role in deciding government bond yield under extreme circumstances.

Analysis framework of "Revised Taylor's Rule"

According to Taylor's original version of the rule, benchmark interest rate should respond to divergences of actual inflation rates from target infla- tion rates and of actual Gross Domestic Product (GDP) from potential GDP: $I = i^* + a(y - y^*) + b(\pi - \pi^*)$. In this equation, i refers to the nominal interest rate, i^* the nominal equilibrium interest rate (when $y = y^*$, $\pi = \pi^*$), y the real output, y^* the target output, π the inflation rate, π^* the target inflation rate, and *a*, *b* positive constants. If the real output > the target output and the inflation rate > the target inflation rate, the nominal interest rate > the nominal equilibrium interest rate.

The "Revised Taylor's Rule" differs from the traditional one in two aspects: first, it has factored in financial system risks as a determinant of interest rate; second, it oversees the long-term interest rate (namely the return rate of long-term government bonds) rather than the short-term interest rate. The revised equation is: $i = i^* + a(y - y^*) + b(\pi - \pi^*) + R$, in which the *R* stands for financial system risks. Specially, *i* is the return rate of 10-year government bond, *y* the real year-on-year GDP, *y** the filtered GDP trend, π the year-on-year CPI, π^* the target inflation rate, and *R* a quantitative index that so far has no proper figure.

Before 2013, traditional Taylor's rule could relatively well stipulate 10-year government bond yield, but in 2013 and 2014, the yield differs greatly from the added-up result of the equation. In the second half of 2013, GDP and CPI both witnessed recovery, but only from 7.5% to 7.9% and 2.2% to 2.7% respectively. While in 2010, GDP and CPI were up from 8% to 12% and −2% to over 2% respectively. Although GDP and CPI of 2013 grew less than that of 2010, the peak of 10-year bill was far over that of 2010 and 2011. Growth and inflation gap are not the reasons for sharp upward trend of government bond. The year 2014 saw little

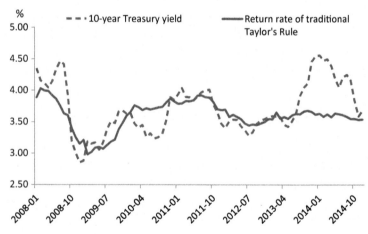

Figure 6.26 Fitted value between the return rate of 10-year government bond and the traditional Taylor's Rule. (Citation: WIND)

change in GDP and CPI, yet 10-year government bond has fallen sharply, even close to the added-up result of traditional Taylor's rule. Why?

At the end of 2013, I suggested a revised Taylor's rule for the yield of long-term government bond, which takes the risks in financial system into account.

Government bonds are generally considered risk-free. Why should we take risks into consideration? In the chapter concerning interest rate liberalization, I have explained that when establishing a large financial market, money market and other financial markets are linked, so the money market reflects the country's interest rate. Heavy soft budget constraint, failure of risk-based pricing, and asset price bubble narrow the interest rate gap between money market and high-risk areas, hence drive up money market rates, and the trend will transmit to the bond market. There are two paths of transmission: first, capital black hole is tied to the money market by non-standard bond assets, etc. Therefore, when the creditors have a greater appetite for risks, demand in the money market will increase, interest rate sensitivity for financing will drop, hence the interest rate will rise, and the interest rate of "risk-free" government bonds will increase; second, government bonds are not "risk-free" as stated, but have the risk of government default. If the financial institutions of a country increase their appetite for risks, the leverage rate becomes too high, so the overall risk rises, and so does the interest rate of government bonds. Similarly, Greek government bonds are risk-free to Greece, but if Greece has solvency problem, the interest rate of its government bonds will surge.

In the second half of 2013, although the economy rebounded only a little, it still facilitated the financial institutions to have a larger appetite for risks. Non-standard bond assets offer tools to link money market with high-yield assets, and this is the number one reason for the rise of money market rates. Besides, over-dependence of financial institutions upon money market debt, pressure on money market caused by short-term debt and maturity mismatch, and financial institutions making loans simultaneously due to homogeneity, all aggravate the upward pressure of money market rates. In 2014, real estate price fell with the economy, and bank bad debt ratio increased significantly; tighter regulations were introduced to control non-standard bond assets, and the preference for risks dropped systematically; therefore, money market rates fell significantly. This is the fundamental reason for the bear market of 2013 and the bull market of 2014.

Financial systemic risk is subject to many factors, which include sovereign default risk, asset price bubble, entity with soft constraint, risk pricing efficiency, financial institutions' risk preference, regulatory policies, etc. (see Table 6.3).

I have illustrated the basic framework for analysis of the bond market. But under some special circumstances, the bond market will be influenced by other factors, mainly supply and demand, politics and people's emotions (see Table 6.4).

Table 6.3   Financial Systemic Risks that directly affect the bond market

Types of financial systemic risk	Explanation
Sovereign default risk	Any risk-free interest rate refers to risk-free rate within a country. If there is sovereign default risk, the yield will surge. A classic example is the European debt crisis and Greece in recent days.
Asset price bubble	The financial market is an interconnected market. When there is an asset price bubble, money in the money market will be invested in it, pushing up the money market interest rate and government bond yield with it.
Entity with soft constraint	A feature of soft-restriction is borrowing money with administrative power and not being sensitive to interest rate. When there is implicit guarantee, some originally risk-averse investors will tend to invest in entities with soft constraint, causing too much total financing demand in the market.
Risk pricing efficiency	When risk pricing is inefficient, credit risk is systematically underestimated, causing credit spread to shrink.
Risk preference	An investor's risk preference determines the share of different risk assets in his portfolio. Assuming that the risk preference of financial institutions in a country undergoes a systematic surge, actual risk in that country will rise substantially, along with the risk-free interest rate. The same conclusion can be deduced from the substantial decrease in demand for risk-free assets.
Regulatory policies	Regulatory policies determine the ceiling of risk preference of financial institutions. Strengthening regulation will drive down risk-free interest rate.

Table 6.4 Impact of three special circumstances besides the revised Taylor's rule on the bond market

Special circumstance	Explanation
Supply and demand	Statistics show that the gap between supply and demand calculated by the scope of issuance and allocation has never had a major influence on the bond market. It only affects the market in extreme cases: 1. dumping resulting from short-term scarcity of capital; 2. sudden injection of money into banks by the central bank; 3. sudden and dramatic increase/decrease in government bond issuing; 4. hot money inflows resulting from opening-up of the market.
Politics	Government behavior conforms to the revised Taylor's rule in the long run, but the timing and route of a policy will exert major influence on the bond market in certain situations. For example, the China Clear Document [No. 149] was issued at a time when the bond market was pulling back and largely intensified the pullback. Yet similar documents had rarely made any impact in a bond bull market before.
Emotions	Behavioral finance exists in every financial market. A classic example is the bond bear market in 2003. And the bond market is heavily reliant on information.

Determinants of Credit Spread

Debenture bond yield = risk-free interest rate + credit spread, so when we analyze the effect of government bond on debenture bond, we should focus on the credit spread. It is generally agreed that credit spread is the interest spread used to make up for the default risk which investors bear. In an advanced bond market, credit spread depends on corporate default rate. In less advanced bond markets such as the Chinese one, credit spread also reflects the liquidity difference between corporate bond and government bond. So for credit spread, there is the following equation:

$$\text{Credit spread} = \text{Corporate default risk premium} + \text{Bond liquidity risk premium.}$$

Corporate default risk premium is dependent on the following factors. First, it mainly depends on a company's current performance, including profitability, debt-to-asset ratio, etc. Most companies are pro-cyclical, meaning that they have better performance and lower default risk during the expansion phase of the economy. So provided that there is no major credit-rating adjustment, a bond with a certain rating will see its credit spread decrease when fundamentals of the economy improve. Second, increasing risk-free interest rate will decrease a company's asset prices and increase its credit spread; but at the same time, increasing risk-free rate will reduce the company's debt burden and thus reduce the credit spread. Therefore, an increase in risk-free rate will have conflicting effects on credit spread, making the end result hard to predict. Third, increasing risk-free rate will lead to economic downturn, lowering a company's expected profitability and thus causing credit spread to expand.

As to liquidity, it mainly refers to liquidity difference of corporate bonds, i.e., difficulty for an investor to liquidate his bond. In a bear market, because of the declined overall interest rate and the downward expectation on yields, liquidity of corporate bond will increase substantially, causing the yield of corporate bond to drop more than that of government bond. In contrast, in a bull market, debenture bond will experience bigger yield increase.

Next, I will verify the above-mentioned theory by analyzing the US and the Chinese debenture bond markets.

First, I will focus on the US debenture bond market. I choose Moody's Aaa Corporate Bond Yield and Baa Corporate Bond Yield to represent debenture bond yield, and use the difference between these and the five-year Treasury Note Yield as credit spreads. Using US five-year Treasury note as the indicator to assess the fundamentals of the US economy is not a very meticulous choice, because US Treasury securities are dependent on both economic growth and inflation. But during non-stagflation period, growth and inflation rarely go in different directions, so the five-year Treasury note is chosen to measure fundamentals for simplicity's sake.

Figure 6.27 clearly shows a rather obvious negative correlation between the credit spread and the five-year Treasury Note Yield for both types of corporate bonds, i.e., when the five-year Treasury Note Yield increased, the credit spreads shrank. There are two explanations. First, an increase in the five-year Treasury Note Yield indicates that fundamentals are gradually improving, thus corporate default risk is down and credit spread is lowered. Second, the increasing risk-free interest rate reduces

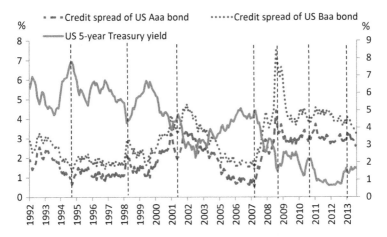

Figure 6.27   Relationship between the US credit spread and the business cycle. (Citation: WIND)

the debt burden of companies and so decreases the credit spread. The decrease in credit spread is bigger than the increase in term spread caused by companies' reduced asset prices. I think that at the beginning of a rate hike/cut, the second explanation has the more prominent effect, because the change in credit spread is closely related to the rate hike/cut. If the fundamentals are the entire cause, there should not be this fact that almost every turning point of the credit spread correlated with a turning point of Treasury bond yield. Yet in the long run, the fundamentals may be the main factor. For example, from 2002 to 2007, the US economy was gradually improving, companies' debt-paying ability was improved and so the credit spread should decrease. Rate hike of the Fed began only in June 2004, whereas the credit spread already began to decrease in 2002, still within the Fed's rate-cutting period. Therefore, what happened in this period cannot be explained by saying that an increasing risk-free rate would reduce credit spread. In conclusion, there is a negative correlation between the credit spread and the Treasury bond yield in the US, and the explanation for this is that corporate performance changes with the business cycle, and that the discount rate, affected by the changing risk-free rate, influences companies' debt burden.

For the Chinese debenture bond market, I distinguish between 3 types of bonds: the first is AA+ and higher; the second is AA; and the third is AA− and below. The credit spread of these 3 types of debenture bonds

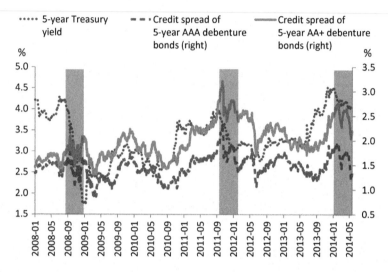

Figure 6.28   Credit spread of high-rating Chinese debenture bonds. (Citation: WIND)

differ from each other. To be more specific, for the first type (AA+ and higher), there is an obvious positive correlation between the credit spread and the government bond yield, i.e., the credit spread shrank when government bond yield decreased. During every economic downturn (corporate default risk would increase substantially, including the time between August and October 2008), the credit spread shrank as government bond yield decreased. There has been only one obvious exception: between October and December 2008 (when the financial crisis had the most severe impact on China), the credit spread expanded while government bond yield decreased.

For the second type (AA), there is a more complex relationship between the credit spread and government bond yield. Most of the time, the credit spread and government bond yield were in positive correlation, just like the first bond type. But when it comes to economic downturns, first, during the 2008 and 2012 economic downturns, the credit spread and government bond yield were in a negative correlation, i.e., credit-free rate decreased while credit spread expanded; second, in the first half of 2014, the credit spread shrank as government bond yield decreased. These two economic downturns demonstrated different changes in the credit spread.

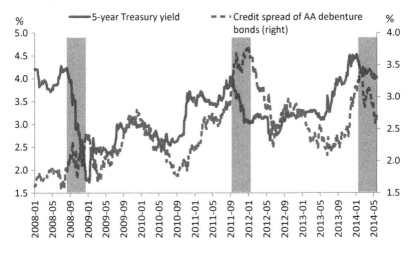

Figure 6.29   Credit spread of AA Chinese debenture bonds. (Citation: WIND)

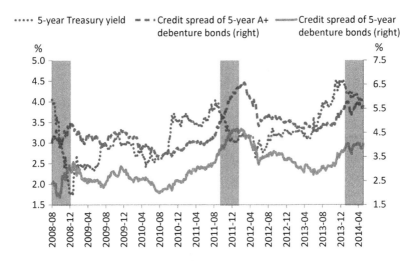

Figure 6.30   Credit spread of low-rating Chinese debenture bonds. (Citation: WIND)

For the third type (AA− and below), the credit spread displays new differences. Most of the time, the credit spread correlated positively with government bond yield, same as the first two types. During downward periods, first, during the 2008 and 2012 economic downturns, the credit spread displayed negative correlation with government bond yield, i.e., the credit spread expanded while risk-free rate decreased, same as the second type of bonds; second, during the 2014 downturn, the credit spread did not shrink as government bond yield dropped, instead it expanded, which was different from the second type of bonds.

To sum up, credit spread in China differs substantially from that in the US, and also has great differences with general credit risk pricing. If credit spread merely depicted credit risk, then during the 3 economic downturns in 2008, 2012, and 2014, credit spread would have expanded as companies' debt-paying ability weakened and their credit risk subsequently rose. That is not what happened. Table 6.5 summarizes the above-mentioned features of credit spread in China. In general, the credit spread of high-rating debenture bonds mainly depends on these bonds' liquidity premium. As to lower-rating debenture bonds, during smooth or upward period, their credit spread also largely depends on liquidity premium, but in a downward period, the determinant will be the credit risk. The degree of influence of credit risk premium varies according to the degree and causes of economic downturns.

Besides the general rules mentioned above, there are certain special occasions in the Chinese bond market. The first is financial crisis. If a financial crisis emerges and causes economic downturn, the default risk of all companies will surge. Then government bonds' advantage of enabling

Table 6.5   Determinant of credit spread in the Chinese bond market

	Benchmark yield increases	Benchmark yield decreases	
		Smooth economy	Obvious economic downturn
AA+ and higher	Bond liquidity risk as determinant, credit spread expands	Bond liquidity risk as determinant, credit spread shrinks	Bond liquidity risk as determinant, credit spread shrinks
AA			Downward scope as determinant
AA− and lower			Corporate credit risk as determinant, credit spread expands

investors to avoid risk becomes more prominent, causing the credit spread of debenture bonds, including high-rating ones, to expand. For example, when the financial crisis broke out between October and December 2008, the credit spread of all debenture bonds (including AAA ones) was amplified, similar to when the financial crisis broke out in the US. Second, short-term liquidity shock: If there is a short-term liquidity shock but not a long-term liquidity problem, e.g., the "6.20" incident last year, financial institutions will solve short-term liquidity crunch by dumping government bonds, which have the lowest yield, forcing credit spread to shrink. But when the market discovers the liquidity crunch to be a long-term problem, the advantage of government bonds in terms of liquidity will become more prominent. That is why in the second half of 2013, bonds of all ratings saw their credit spread expand substantially.

In my opinion, there are two main reasons for the difference in the credit spread of Chinese debenture bonds and that of the US debenture bonds.

• Credit risk in the US mainly results from material default. There are lots of material defaults in the US, so credit risk pricing is based on the material default rate; yet material corporate defaults are extremely rare in China, with no default precedent among middle-to-high-rating bonds, so there is a certain degree of expectation on rigid payment. That is to say, in the US, corporate credit risk is the determinant of credit spread, whereas in China, corporate credit risk has a far less impact. Only when there is obvious economic downturn, will the expectation on rigid payment change.

• Chinese corporate bonds have a relatively low liquidity. The depth and width of the US bond market far exceed those of the Chinese market, and the liquidity of US debenture bonds is much greater than that of the Chinese ones. So in the US, it is unnecessary to calculate the liquidity risk of bonds, whose liquidity risk premium can be ignored in most cases. But in China, inactive bonds are very common, forcing Chinese investors to take bonds' liquidity into consideration. This problem is especially prevalent in a bear market.

Let us review the three factors which affect a company's default risk premium in theory: First is the company's current performance with respect to its debt-paying ability, and the other two are expectations on the company's debt-paying ability. I think that in terms of debenture bonds, Chinese investors mostly consider a company's current debt-paying ability rather than the expectations on its future debt-paying ability. If expectations were the focus, in an economic downturn with lower interest rates, expected future higher profitability would cause the credit spread to shrink. Yet in reality, the credit spread of middle-to-low-rating bonds expands as interest rates fall in economic downturns. In addition, if credit risk pricing is based on expectations, less qualified companies would receive stronger expectations on future improvements of profitability, and therefore would see their credit spread shrink more. But in fact, the lower the rating of a bond, the bigger the expansion of its credit spread. Therefore, credit spread in the Chinese debenture bond market is determined by current performance, not future expectation. The conclusion is that the influence of the central bank's monetary policies on debenture bonds mainly comes from their influence on the risk-free interest rate, and that credit spread is under little influence of monetary policies but is basically determined by the current business cycle.

Chapter Seven

The Central Bank in Big Data Era

Big data, a hot word of China in 2014, is ubiquitous in all walks of life, from Internet industry to weather forecast, from politics to military business. However, the application of big data in macroeconomic regulation is rarely mentioned and that in economic management is not clearly defined. In fact, not only does big data transform the real economy, but also it has a profound impact on the macroeconomic regulation. The United States has long adopted the big data strategy and Britain took the lead in introducing big data into monetary policy. So, why has great attention been attached to big data in the macroeconomic regulation by developed countries? What are the new features of macroeconomic regulation with big data? And what can China learn from others in macroeconomic regulation with big data? In this chapter, I will analyze the influence of big data on monetary policy to answer these questions.

I believe that the big data era has initiated the transformation from industrialization era to intelligence era, a leap of human society. The improvement of production capacity of human beings through big data technology can be much more compared to industrial revolution. In theory, the prosperity of big data era depends on the development of data storage, processing and data mining technology. The great development of computer technology and data storage has laid the foundation for the big data era. In nature, big data means the increasing, common and sensitive connection between everything. Big data has the following characteristics: (1) in terms of structured data, real-time tracking data replaces dot distributed financial statement data, providing a more direct, dynamic and accurate image of a company; (2) in terms of the unstructured data, quantitative behavior analysis is feasible. The technology is widely used in bank credit risk assessment and big data asset allocation, improving financial efficiency and lowering financial risk.

In big data era, the central bank will develop to version 4.0. I assume that the first generation of central banks is central banks in gold standard era, the second is central banks using quantitative control, the third is central banks regulating in price rule and the fourth generation is central banks in big data era. We can see the following changes. First, the central bank changes its signal that are based on when making decisions from time-point data of financial statements to real-time dynamic data, and it also changes the regulation mechanism. Second, the central bank begins to take advantage of behavioral finance and unstructured data. Last, the monetary policy simulation and virtual economic laboratory became possible. In such cases, humans are prevented from the consequences of policy mistakes by improving the possibility of successful anticipation and correction of mistakes. The People's Bank of China should attach great importance to the new characteristics of the big data era, striving for the transformation from the second generation to the fourth one.

In the first section of this chapter, we will introduce the revolutionary impact of big data on the real economy, as well as the experience of employing big data in other countries. In section two, we are going to talk about the profound influence of big data on financial industry. In section three, we analyze the characteristics and application of macroeconomic regulation with big data, and also the features of central banks of version 4.0.

SECTION ONE: OVERVIEW OF BIG DATA

In 2014, a hot word "big data" seems ubiquitous in the press. In different industries, including E-commerce, search engines, banking, Internet finance and communication industries, the concept of big data was highly discussed in terms of further upgradation. According to the research conducted by Kearney, more than 45% of companies took measures related to business intelligence or big data in 2013 and 2014.

In such a big data era, the public may still be unclear about the definition and the use of big data. Though we will not talk about big data separately, because this book focuses on the monetary policy, we cannot move to the topic of monetary policy in big data era without a clear definition and direction of big data. So, in this section, we will introduce big data and its impact on human society from a macro perspective.

Why is Big Data so Hot Today?

The concept of big data was first mentioned in the 1980s, but did not become popular until the rise of Internet finance after 2009. The accumulation and propagation of data are the foundation of the emergence of big data. The publishing of *Big Data* written by Cukier triggered the popularity of big data in China. I believe that most readers have one questions — cool it may sound, but will the accumulating data turn a new page of our life? Does the explosive data mean the coming of big data era? And do we really need big data?

In March 2012, the White House Office of Science and Technology Policy launched the Big Data Research and Development Program, and organized an advanced group to coordinate. This suggests that the United States, always in the frontier of human science and technology, has carried out its national big data strategy. In China, many provinces have also launched the big data strategy. For example, Guizhou province and Alibaba Group announced a strategic cooperation framework agreement about cloud computing and big data, contributing to the construction of "Digital Guizhou." The rise of big data seems to provide less developed provinces in the Midwest with opportunities to catch up.

So why did governments pay such attention to big data? We may refer to the Big Data Strategy of the United States to find out this answer. It is mentioned in the Big Data Strategy that the purpose is to improve the ability to extract knowledge and views from massive data, and to promote the development in science and engineering as well. The Defense Department, Department of Homeland Security, NASA and Department of Energy's Office of Science all play important roles in this big data plan. The plan they put forward is not an air castle, but the feasible application of massive and timely data to solve problems in each fields that were difficult to tackle before. The use of big data will significantly accelerate the process of transformation from science and technology to innovation and achievements in the United States.

The Experience from the US: Open Source Data, Unified Data-Backup and Industrial Data Center

From the national level, in big data era, if a country wants to win a place in the era of intelligence, national big data strategy is indispensable. This is because big data asks for massive data, while few companies or institutions have the access to mass data, except the country or some large Internet companies. Data without national unified background supports is incomplete, whose effectiveness also is greatly reduced. In China, the application of big data we heard about today is only exercised in individual companies, namely Baidu and Alibaba. Without the important support of the country, big data in China is only a dream rather than a feasible project.

The government of the Unites States set up an open data platform, data.gov, sharing 50 kinds of data and releasing the API index as well as many application programs and software tools. Moreover, the United States opened the source of data.gov together with India, providing developers around the world with managed code for usage or modification to their needs. Thus, it is possible for the US to take advantage of the global intellectual resources to solve the problems in society, science and technology, boosting the development of the US.

From the industry level, the collection and unity of data are also necessary in the development of big data. In many industries, information is scattered and non-standard, which makes concentrated standardized information very important. For example, the US is trying to build a broader credit framework in the medical industry, gathering the health data with different resources and levels of privacy. In China, commercial banks have begun to jointly establish individual credit data platforms, making the credit information of borrowers more transparent among banks and providing more accurate credit evaluation. The establishment of data center is also useful in other areas, such as education, health, retail sales and so on.

From the technical level, the coming of the big data era is based on the rapid improvement of data processing and data mining, which means the development of high-capacity computers and integrated circuit is the precondition. In fact, cloud computing and the Internet are heavily dependent on the intelligentization of data processing and data mining.

The Future of Big Data: Reconstruction of the Human Society in Intelligence Era

We have introduced much about the background information of big data, but I think we should pay more attention on the future of big data.

With the advent of big data era, mass data can be acquired timely, making the virtual reality technology possible. The great progress of virtual reality compared to the real reality is the feasible application of 4D. With the breakthrough of 4D technology, 4D printing, 4D weather forecast, and 4D imaging will embrace a new opportunity. In addition, in big data era, the way people deal with problems changes a lot. In the age of human brain surpassing computers, people decide according to their own logic deduction and logic judgment. But with the virtual reality technology based on big data, we could make decisions according to the conclusion of computer simulation. If so, humans are able to achieve great breakthroughs in key areas that have not been explored, such as quantum mechanics, frontiers of medical science and so on. I assert that the advent of big data era means the transformation of human society from industrial era to the new intelligence era.

We could see that big data will transform human society from 3D society to 4D society, from a relatively closed society to a comprehensive integrated society, from industrialization to intelligentization, serving as a key to the future society. Surely, big data also will bring us several problems, such as privacy protection, the risk of intelligentization out of control, data war and so on. But I do believe that just as the industrial era, starting with pain and disaster but ending in a new epoch, the big data era will also lead us to a bright future.

SECTION TWO: BIG DATA AND FINANCIAL MARKET

The reason why we need to study the application of big data in financial industry is that there are weaknesses in our traditional logic analysis. For instance, we take advantages of several observational indexes, but these indicators may contradict each other. In the first half of 2014, the index of Industrial Added Value kept a rapid growth rate, while PMI was below 50 constantly. Because of the chaos in logic analysis, we need more data to support our judgment on economic growth.

Big Data and Financial are Naturally Inseparable From Each Other

For financial industry, data is the basis. Thus, the access to data can even become the classification standard of different eras of finance. According to the frequency and accuracy of data, we can divide the financial history into different eras. Before the industrial revolution, due to the lack of investment objects and related data, there was no real financial industry. With the accumulation of data, as well as the development of econometrics, people had a growing understanding of financial investments and economic operation, which still cannot meet the need of high-frequency investment. In big data era, with the transaction frequency gradually matching the arithmetic frequency, high frequency investment tends to be feasible.

It is suggested that high-frequency trading strategies are closely related to big data. In China, high-frequency quantitative trading is rare but profitable by means of constantly adjusting the trading strategy and improving running speed. We can see that high-frequency strategy is profitable due to arbitrage resulting from imperfection of financial system and the lack of data application. In big data era, the programmed high frequency data, as well as the data mining technology and prediction function, will open a new page for financial investments.

On the other side, big data is widely used in financial industry. Globally, big data has contributed to three big financial innovations — credit risk analysis, high-frequency trading and social emotion analysis.

In terms of investment scale with big data in China, application in financial industry ranks the third, just after Internet and telecom industry. As for the comprehensive value potential of big data application, insurance industry ranks second, only after information technology industry. However, the application of big data in the financial industry is still limited to credit risk analysis, the most important and strongest business of the banking industry, including operation optimization, precision marketing and risk control. When it comes to high-frequency trading, due to the conflict between the system design of financial market in China and the concept of high-frequency trading, such as the $T + 1$ rule in the stock market, the development of high-frequency trading is so hard that related technology is far behind the global average. In social emotion analysis, some companies have started to analyze and apply the data about behavior and emotion of Internet users.

The Concept of Big Data Finance

Logically, the concept of big data finance is very simple. People make statistical analysis about big data, and find the commonality and apply that to individuals, while the mass data greatly expands the samples. It is undeniable that the current age is the best time for big data technology to speed up. The main reason is that we are entering an era of connectivity. Thanks to Internet, everything is connected, resulting in a more prompt and profound butterfly effect. For example, the default in photovoltaic industry in China will affect the price of copper quickly in the global market. Therefore, the analysis of different relationships and reality, simulation becomes more and more necessary and important.

Before the application of big data, spurious regression and the excluded variables problem are common in econometrics. Insufficient data may lead to missing possible regression factor, while too much data may affect the over-accuracy of the model. We introduced a variety of tests to judge the existence of spurious regression. Unit Root Test is a case in point, but it can prove the conclusion only technologically and not logically. Big data provides mass sample, which can be tested to see whether the relationship holds. Besides, as there is no accuracy problem in big data prediction, a lot of econometric work could be replaced and some will be deepened.

This is just an example of the functions of big data. Apart from the further use of structured data than econometrics, big data has the advantage in collecting and analyzing unstructured data, such as geographic information, science and technology innovation, and policy documents. The use of such information drove the creation of digital map, driverless cars and other technology products. In the field of finance, the generally used unstructured information is the change of emotion, especially the change of investor emotion. In the United States, constructing the portfolio by the big data strategy of emotion analysis based on data on social network has replaced the index fund to a certain extent, with great profit. In China, the performance of big data fund is similar to index fund, without any positive alpha. I think the failure of big data in investment analysis in China results from the different user groups. In China, the Internet, especially the social network, focuses on low-end group, while the deciding force of stock market is high-end users. Thus, it takes some time to apply big data to investment analysis effectively in China.

The Future of Big Data Finance

We talked about the current development of big data finance in China. But in fact, the future of big data finance is far more promising. A significant change that we will experience is behavioral finance which will be one of the mainstream finance. If we say that finance and data are good friends, behavioral finance and big data are just like a pair of twin brothers. Behavioral finance is considered as a peripheral laboratory discipline, for emotion is difficult to describe. Historically, behavior finance can be traced back to the 1980s, in a stock model designed by Robert Schiller. In that model, three variables were considered, cash flow of investment project, estimated corporate capital cost and the reaction of stock market to investment, that is, the market sentiment. But due to the lack of big data, market sentiment was hard to quantify. Thus, unstructured data, namely behavioral finance, did not make much progress since firstly introduced in the 1980s.

In big data era, with the support of much more data, the improvement of data mining and the popularity of social network, a data pool about investor sentiment has been established, through which we can get the high-frequency variable of investor sentiment, promoting behavioral finance as one of the mainstream finance.

For finance, big data plays a more important role through its basic function. The rich and timely data makes it possible to time track and refresh data. In such cases, investors conduct company analysis not only based on the monthly or quarterly published balance sheet. Investors could gain a better understanding about the company's financial situation through the high-frequency sales data, comments on social network and other information disclosure. The quantification processing of such structured and unstructured data will equip investments with data analysis. In other words, the evolution of company financial statements in big data era will lead financial investments to a new quantitative era.

Big data also does good to credit reconstruction and Small and Medium Enterprises (SME) financing difficulties. The application of big data finance in credit and loan will greatly change the current banking operation. For banks, the key problem is bad debts, while the past record of business operation can only work as a reference for future possibility of bad debts, not accurately. Similarly, the lack of data record of entrepreneurial enterprises prevents banks from benefiting from the development of venture enterprises. This leads to a dilemma that most capital flows to traditional industries and the emerging industries, which need money most, have no access to capital support. In big data era, we can get more information besides the financial statements to make investment decisions. Thus, big data will greatly boost emerging industries, good to the improvement of the overall economy.

SECTION THREE: BIG DATA AND THE CENTRAL BANK OF VERSION 4.0

I think the development of central banks can be divided into four generations. The first generation is the gold standard era. With the absence of monetary policy tools, the central banks could do nothing about the economy. In the second generation, the central banks took advantage of quantitative control tools. In the third generation, the central banks regulated the macroeconomy in price rule. In the second and third generation, the accuracy of macro regulation was gradually improved, but the time lag in monetary policy was inevitable, so that the theory of monetary policy consistency was quite popular. The common characteristic of these two generations is that the structural adjustment is with high difficulty but low precision. The central bank of version 4.0 is the monetary authority under the great development of information technology. It is capable of combing monetary policy operation with emerging technologies, conducting monetary policy simulation to promote more accurate and real-time monetary policies. In this generation, the development of information technology shortening time lag, and the creation of new monetary policy tools based on unstructured data and high-frequency structured data, make structural adjustment easier; the central bank tends to adopt structural monetary policies.

Before talking about monetary policy in big data era, we need to emphasize that the monetary policy we refer to is the overall concept. Monetary policies can be divided into two categories, one is the regular money market intervention, and the other is the overall policies that have effect on economic growth and inflation. In this section, we refer to the latter one.

Higher Sensitivity of Policy Response and Shorter Time Lag

In the new era, the traditional monetary policy is confronting huge reformation in the way of thinking, the responding speed and monetary policy tools. Before talking about the reformation, we take a review about the way of thinking in traditional monetary policy. First, the central bank makes a judgment on current macroeconomic operation according to the monthly or quarterly data; then the Monetary Policy Committee (MPC) meeting is held to discuss about monetary policy. To avoid making mistakes, the decisions of MPC are reported to different levels for approvals. Usually, it takes two quarters for the central bank to confirm an economic downturn, not to mention the uncertain time lag in policy operation. Affected by the internal and external lags, the implementation of monetary policy is lagged far behind the changing economic situation. This is why Monetarist are against discretionary monetary policy with long and uncertain time lag, the monetary policy is unable to stabilize the economy, and may cause adverse effects.

So can the time lag be shortened in big data era? The answer is yes. On one hand, the internal lag of monetary policy in big data era is greatly shortened. Take money market for example. As we know, the capital liquidity is influenced by multiple factors, including bank credit, deposit reserve payment, levered allocation of non-standard assets, foreign exchange inflows and outflows, and the payment of fiscal deposits. It takes the central bank nearly a month to get these data. But in big data era, as the overnight lending data in interbank market is open, timely and with high frequency, the central bank has direct access to these data, resulting in greatly shortened time lag in liquidity judgment. Overall, the high frequency of macroeconomic data and easy access to these data help to shorten the internal judgment time lag dramatically.

On the other hand, the external time lag of monetary policy in big data era is also further shortened. We believe that in big data era, operations on money market will neither be decided by MPC nor be approved by different levels. First of all, the market capital liquidity is not so important for macroeconomy. Secondly, high-frequency data provides us with several indicators to observe the consequences of our policy. Lastly, the policy can be quickly adjusted through a reverse operation, greatly lowering the operation risk of monetary policy. In conclusion, the abundant observation indexes as well as the higher sensitivity of policy response make the time-consuming reporting and approvals unnecessary, reducing the time lag in policy operation. Thus, the shorter judgment time lag and operation time lag help monetary policy to work efficiently and effectively.

The Complement of Industrial Data and the Precise Policy Guidance

Traditional economic databases are unable to provide data support for peripheral enterprises, such as service industry and the SMEs. However, big data makes it possible to establish data center for each industry, providing monthly, 10-day or even weekly tracking observation about the present and the future of the industry. Under such circumstances, precise monetary policy guidance and structured operation are feasible.

Through the description of the 2015 economic situation, we can actually have a more clear understanding about the problems faced by traditional monetary policy. In 2014, the economy was confronting a structural decline, heavy industry and chemical industry stuck in business distress, SMEs facing operation deterioration, and service industry being the drive of the economy. In the process of structural transformation, our monetary policy faces some difficulties.

First, for the service industry and SMEs, we face the absence of observation index to judge the development of these industries. In the service industry, we now have the data of the PMI index of the service sector and the proportion of service industry in GDP growth. But the former is too volatile and with too weak trend that is pointless in future prediction; the latter is with too low frequency to have actual effect. As for SMEs, we have no measurable data at all. The only data the central bank may have includes the credit scale of commercial banks to SMEs and the interest rate of P2P industry after the rise of Internet finance. With the lack of the observation index reflecting these industries, the monetary policy is very risky.

Second, for the unbalanced economic structure, we lack structural monetary policy tools and precise channels. In 2014, the economy was not balanced. Innovative enterprises were emerging, badly in need of further credit support but with high risk. And real estate industry and the traditional heavy industry were stuck in a dilemma, where excessive stimulus may cause over-capacity but lack of stimulus may lead to depression. Under such circumstances, structural monetary policy is urgent. The People's Bank of China adopted some structural monetary policies, including Medium-term Lending Facility (MLF) and Standing Lending Facility (SLF), yet with little effect. The discounted effect was the result of lacking precise data and channels. For example, if we have accurate quantitative data about SMEs, the money by MLF and SLF can be used efficiently, instead of being used to raise the leverage of banks. Surely, as we have no precise delivery channels, such as exclusive SMEs banks and special bonds, problems will not be solved even if the detailed industry observation indexes are prepared, but at least the effect of structural monetary policy can be greatly improved.

Big data may solve this problem. I prefer to compare the relationship between monetary policy before and after the rise of big data to the difference between Chinese and western medicine. Due to the lack of modern scientific instruments and accurate data, Chinese medicine adopts the method of overall treatment, regardless of the damage brought to other organs, while western medicine can treat the targeted organs. In big data era, we believe that monetary policy can also realize the structural operation. Thus, each industry will face the best opportunity and our economy will develop healthily and sustainably.

Virtual Reality Technology and Monetary Policy Simulation

Now let us come to the big data and virtual reality technology, as well as its possible influence on monetary policy. Usually, virtual reality technology refers to creating a 3D virtual world by computer simulation. Currently, it is generally used in business service, to provide consumers with real images, improving the consumer experience and promoting sales. The virtual reality we talk about here is to reflect the impacts that monetary regulation has on each industry through the designed model.

This is monetary policy simulation. A monetary policy laboratory is expected to be established to reflect possible policy influence and to reduce the possibility of policy failure leading to economic disaster. For those situations that are not covered by simulation, thanks to high-frequency data, it is easy for the central bank to adjust policies. After the implementation of the policy, the central bank can observe the real time change of economy, conduct quick hedging response once unexpected things happen, and thus can reduce the negative impact of monetary policy on economy.

Bibliography

Bernanke, Ben, S. 2014. *The Federal Reserve and the financial crisis*, eds. Shusong Ba, Jian Chen. Princeton University Press.

Deng, Haiqing. 2013. *Interest rate liberalization: Breaking out China's debt predicament*. China Sodial Sciences Press.

Friedman, Milton, and Anna J. Schwartz. 2009. *A monetary history of the United States, 1867–1960*, eds. Shusong Ba, Jinsong Wang. Peking University Press.

Li, Bin, and Ge Wu. 2014. *Credit creation, money and economic structure*. China Financial Publishing House.

Sun, Guofeng. 2012. *China's financial reforms*. China Financial Publishing House.

Wang, Jian. 2013. *The Real Federal Reserve*. Zhejiang University Press.

Wang, Yang. 2008. *China's monetary policy framework*. China Financial & Economic Publishing House

Zhang, Jianhua. 2012. *Interest rate liberalization*. China Machine Press.

Zhang, Xiaohui. 2012. *China monetary policy*. China Financial Publishing House.

Index

209

Printed in the United States
By Bookmasters